James Payn

English Sacred Lyrics

James Payn

English Sacred Lyrics

ISBN/EAN: 9783744796392

Printed in Europe, USA, Canada, Australia, Japan

Cover: Foto ©Thomas Meinert / pixelio.de

More available books at **www.hansebooks.com**

ARBOR SCIENTIÆ
ARBOR VITÆ

LONDON

KEGAN PAUL, TRENCH & CO

MDCCCLXXXIIII

CONTENTS.

CONTENTS.   ix

INTRODUCTION.

IN adding another collection of sacred poetry to those already existing, a somewhat different aim has been proposed than that of many previous gatherers in the same field. There is here no attempt to frame a hymn book; in fact, the proportion of true hymns in the volume is unusually small. Nor is there any plan of presenting one system of doctrine, so as to include or exclude any opinions whatever. Neither, again, are great poets to be found here because they are great, nor lesser poets omitted because their names are little known, —the simple test has been whether the poems satisfied certain requirements, not in any degree who may have written them.

It has been required that they satisfy the demands of lyrical form and expression, and to be infused with religious emotion. And it may be frankly allowed that both these are matters wherein tastes differ, nor can the sentiments of the heart be analysed with nice accuracy, especially when concerned with religion. But no pains have been spared during some years to search through all the best religious poems of our literature, and the lyrics here presented are what seem best to the editor, who trusts that at least he has gathered what may please and interest others.

No doubt many will find that some favourite poems are omitted, but the reasons for their omission will usually be plain. The longer Ode finding no place in the scheme, Milton on the Nativity was left aside with reluctance ; it would have been but a purple patch, incongruous with the rest of the volume. Mrs. Barbauld's ' God of my life and author of my days,' however lyrical in feeling here and there, is shut out by its form, as are many beautiful sonnets. Yet in one or two cases the lyrical feeling has appeared so strong as to compel inclusion in spite of the deficiency of form.

It at first seemed strange that only a few hymns could be gathered in, but on reflection it is strange that any should be included. For the essence of a hymn is that it reflect the feelings of the many, not the devotional cry which at any given time can appeal to but a few. If any will take the popular hymnology, and criticise it calmly, they will find that, with rare exceptions, those hymns are the most popular which are least expressive of the deeper spiritual feelings. They owe to their associated music, or sometimes to their commonplace refrain, which none can misunderstand, their charm when sung, a charm which evaporates if they be read. The modern developments of hymnology in both its dogmatic extremes will afford too many instances to need here any special application.

The one fact which has become increasingly clear during the growth of this selection is the great similarity of the effects of religious emotion on the mind of whoso is touched by it. Catholic and Protestant, Orthodox and Evangelical, Christian and Positivist speak in much the same strain, even if the words are different, as Gretchen in ' Faust ' found that her lover's confession of faith, different as was the phrase, was very like what her priest had taught her. This is not said to undervalue or minimise differences, but simply to point out that when the soul goes out of self towards that which is not self, there is a great sameness underlying all the variations both of the object and the expression. And the lyrics included in the present volume are those which in the long range of English literature seem most fitly to represent the attitude of the soul to that which is above and beyond.

ENGLISH SACRED LYRICS.

ANNE ASKEW,
1529—1546.

LINES IN PRISON.

LIKE as the armed knight,
　Appointed to the field,
With this world will I fight,
　And faith shall be my shield.

Faith is that weapon strong,
　Which will not fail at need ;
My foes therefore among
　Therewith will I proceed.

As it is had in strength
　And force of Christ his way,
It will prevail at length
　Though all the devils say nay.

Faith in the Fathers old
　Obtained righteousness,
Which maketh me so bold
　To fear no world's distress.

B

I now rejoice in heart,
  And hope bids me do so,
For Christ will take my part
  And ease me of my woe.

Thou say'st, Lord, whoso knock
  To them wilt thou attend ;
Undo therefore the lock,
  And thy strong power down send.

More enemies I have
  Than hairs to crown my head,
Let them not me deprave,
  But fight thou in my stead.

On thee my care I cast,
  For all their cruel spite ;
I set not by their haste,
  For thou art my delight.

I am not she that list
  My anchor to let fall
For every drizzling mist,
  My ship's substantial.

Not oft use I to write
  In prose, nor yet in rime ;

Yet will I show one sight
   That I saw in my time.

I saw a royal throne
   Where justice should have sit,
But in her stead was one
   Of moody cruel wit.

Absorbed was righteousness
   As by a raging flood ;
Satan in fierce excess
   Sucked up the guiltless blood.

Then thought I—Jesu, Lord !
   When thou shalt judge us all,
Hard is it to record
   On these men what will fall.

Yet Lord, I thee desire,
   For what they do to me
Let them not taste the hire
   Of their iniquity.

II.

ANON.

? 1530.

Quoted in ' Dives and Pauper,' 1536.

WHEN I think on Jesu's blood
   That he shed upon the rood,
      I let tears smart :
Who of men can be unkind,
If Christ's blood he hath in mind,
      Entirely in his heart.

Sweet Jesu Christ ! what is thy guilt,
That thou thus for me art spilt,
      Flower of unlothfulness ?
I a thief am, and thou diest ;
I am guilty, thou abyest
      All my wickedness.

Why gavest thou so much for thine ?
What winnest thou with thy hard pine
      Rich in bliss above ?
Love thy heart so deep has sought,
That pain of death doth let thee nought,
      Of man to win the love.

III.

NICHOLAS BRETON,
1542—? 1626.

HYMN.

WHEN the angels all are singing,
All of glory ever springing,
In the ground of high heaven's graces,
Where all virtues have their places :
O that my poor soul were near them,
With an humble heart to hear them !

Then should Faith in Love's submission,
Joying but in Mercy's blessing,
Where that sins are in remission,
Sing the joyful soul's confessing,
Of her comforts high commending,
All in glory, never ending.

But, ah wretched sinful creature !
How should the corrupted nature
Of this wicked heart of mine,
Think upon that love divine,
That doth tune the angels' voices,
While the host of heaven rejoices ?

No, the song of deadly sorrow,
In the night that hath no morrow,
And their pains are never ended,
That have heavenly powers offended,
    Is more fitting to the merit
    Of my foul infected spirit.

Yet while Mercy is removing
All the sorrows of the loving,
How can Faith be full of blindness,
To despair of Mercy's kindness;
    While the hand of heaven is giving
    Comfort from the ever living?

No, my soul, be no more sorry;
Look unto that life of glory,
Which the grace of Faith regardeth,
And the tears of Love rewardeth:
    Where the soul the comfort getteth,
    That the angels' music setteth.

There when thou art well conducted,
And by heavenly grace instructed,
How the faithful thoughts to fashion
Of a ravished lover's passion,
    Sing with saints to angels nighest,
    Halleluiah in the highest!

FRANCIS KINDLEMARSH,
circa 1550.
' *Paradise of Dainty Devices.*'

IV.

FOR CHRISTMAS DAY.

F ROM Virgin's womb this day did spring,
   The precious seed that only saved man ;
This day let man rejoice and sweetly sing,
   Since on this day salvation first began.
      This day did Christ man's soul from death remove,
      With glorious saints to dwell in heaven above.

This day to man, came pledge of perfect peace,
   This day to man, came love and unity ;
This day man's grief began for to surcease,
   This day did man receive a remedy.
      For each offence and every deadly sin,
      With guilty heart that erst he wandered in.

In Christes flock, let love be surely placed,
   From Christes flock, let concord hate expel ;
Of Christes flock let love be so embraced,
   As we in Christ, and Christ in us may dwell.
      Christ is the author of all unity,
      From whence proceedeth all felicity.

O sing unto this glittering glorious King,
O praise his name let every living thing,
Let heart and voice like bells of silver ring,
The comfort that this day did bring :
    Let lute, let shalm, with sound of sweet delight,
    The joy of Christes birth this day recite.

SIR WALTER RALEIGH,
1552—1618.

V.

*   A HYMN.

R ISE, O my soul, with thy desires to heaven,
     And with divinest contemplation use
Thy time where time's eternity is given,
    And let vain thoughts no more thy thoughts abuse ;
        But down in darkness let them lie :
        So live thy better, let thy worse thoughts die !

And thou, my soul, inspired with holy flame,
    View and review with most regardful eye
That holy cross, whence thy salvation came,
    On which thy Saviour and thy sin did die !
        For in that sacred object is much pleasure,
        And in that Saviour is my life, my treasure.

To thee, O Jesu ! I direct mine eye,
    To thee my hands, to thee my humble knees ;
To thee my heart shall offer sacrifice,
    To thee my thoughts, who my thoughts only sees.
        To thee my self, my self and all I give ;
        To thee I die, to thee I only live !

VI.

HIS PILGRIMAGE.

GIVE me my scallop-shell of quiet,
   My staff of faith to walk upon ;
My scrip of joy, immortal diet ;
My bottle of salvation.
My gown of glory, hope's true gage,
And thus I'll take my pilgrimage.
Blood must be my body's only balmer,
Whilst my soul like a quiet palmer,
Travelleth towards the land of heaven,
No other balm will there be given.
Over the silver mountains,
Where springs the nectar fountains,
There will I kiss the bowl of bliss,
And drink mine everlasting fill
Upon every milken hill.
My soul will be a-dry before,
But after, it will thirst no more.
I'll take them first, to quench my thirst,
   And taste of nectar's suckets,
      At those clear wells
      Where sweetness dwells,
   Drawn up by saints in crystal buckets.
Then by that happy blestful day,

More peaceful pilgrims I shall see,
That have cast off their rags of clay,
And walk apparelled fresh like me,
And when our bodies and all we
Are filled with immortality,
Then the blessed parts we'll travel,
Strewed with rubies thick as gravel,
Ceilings of diamonds, sapphire flowers,
High walls of corals, and pearly bowers.
From thence to heaven's bribeless hall,
Where no corrupted voices brawl,
No conscience molten into gold,
No forged accuser bought or sold,
No cause deferred, no vain spent journey,
For there Christ is the king's attorney,
Who pleads for all without degrees,
And he hath angels, but no fees :
And when the twelve grand million jury
Of our sins, with direful fury,
'Gainst our souls black verdicts give,
Christ pleads his death, and then we live.
Be thou my speaker, taintless pleader,
Unblotted lawyer, true proceeder,
Thou would'st salvation even for alms,
Not with a bribed lawyer's palms.
And this is mine eternal plea,
To him that made heaven, earth and sea,

That since my flesh must die so soon,
And want a head to dine next noon,
Just at the stroke, when my veins start and spread,
Set on my soul an everlasting head.
Then am I ready, like a palmer fit,
To tread those blest paths which before I writ.
Of death and judgment, heaven and hell ;
Who oft doth think, must needs die well.

VII.

VERSES FOUND IN HIS BIBLE IN THE
GATEHOUSE AT WESTMINSTER.

E VEN such is time, which takes in trust
    Our youth, our joys, and all we have,
And pays us nought but age and dust,
Which in the dark and silent grave,
When we have wandered all our ways,
Shuts up the story of our days ;
And from which grave, and earth, and dust,
The Lord shall raise me up I trust.

SIR PHILIP SIDNEY,
1554—1586.

VIII.

PSALM XXIII. DOMINUS REGIT ME.

THE Lord, the Lord my shepherd is,
    And so can never I
        Taste misery.
He rests me in green pastures his ;
    By waters still and sweet
        He guides my feet.

He me revives, leads me the way
    Which righteousness doth take,
        For his name's sake :
Yea, though I should through valleys stray
    Of death's dark shade, I will
        No whit fear ill.

For thou, dear Lord, thou me besetst,
    Thy rod and thy staff be
        To comfort me :
Before me thou a table setst,
    Even when foes' envious eye
        Doth it espy.

Thou oil'st my head, thou fill'st my cup ;
Nay, more, thou endless good,
Shalt give me food :
To thee, I say, ascended up
Where thou, the Lord of all,
Dost hold thy hall.

IX.

ROBERT SOUTHWELL,
1560—1595.

A CHILD MY CHOICE.

LET folly praise that fancy loves, I praise and love
    that child
Whose heart no thought, whose tongue no word, whose
    hand no deed defiled.
I praise him most, I love him best, all praise and love is
    his ;
While him I love, in him I live, and cannot live amiss.
Love's sweetest mark, laud's highest theme, man's most
    desired light,
To love him life, to leave him death, to live in him
    delight.
He mine by gift, I his by debt, thus each to other due,
First friend he was, best friend he is, all times will try
    him true.
Though young, yet wise ; though small, yet strong ;
    though man, yet God he is ;
As wise he knows, as strong he can, as God he loves to
    bliss.
His knowledge rules, his strength defends, his love doth
    cherish all ;

His birth our joy, his life our light, his death our end of
thrall.
Alas ! he weeps, he sighs, he pants, yet do his angels
sing ;
Out of his tears, his sighs and throbs, doth bud a joyful
spring.
Almighty Babe, whose tender arms can force all foes to
fly,
Correct my faults, protect my life, direct me when I die !

X.

NEW HEAVEN, NEW WAR.

COME to your heaven, you heavenly choirs !
Earth hath the heaven of your desires ;
Remove your dwelling to your God,
A stall is now his best abode ;
Since men their homage do deny,
Come, angels, all their fault supply.

His chilling cold doth heat require,
Come, seraphims, in lieu of fire.
This little ark no cover hath,
Let cherubs' wings his body swath ;
Come, Raphael, this babe must eat,
Provide our little Tobie meat.

Let Gabriel be now his groom,
That first took up his earthly room ;
Let Michael stand in his defence,
Whom love hath linked to feeble sense ;
Let graces rock, when he doth cry,
And angels sing his lullaby.

The same you saw in heavenly seat,
Is he that now sucks Mary's teat ;
Agnise your King a mortal wight,
His borrowed weed lets not your sight ;
Come, kiss the manger where he lies ;
That is your bliss above the skies.

This little Babe so few days old,
Is come to rifle Satan's fold ;
All hell doth at his presence quake,
Though he himself for cold do shake ;
For in this weak unarmed wise
The gates of hell he will surprise.

With tears he fights and wins the field,
His naked breast stands for a shield,
His battering shots are babish cries,
His arrows, looks of weeping eyes,
His martial ensigns, cold and need,
And feeble flesh his warrior's steed.

C

His camp is pitched in a stall,
His bulwark but a broken wall,
The crib his trench, hay-stalks his stakes,
Of shepherds he his muster makes ;
And thus, as sure his foe to wound,
The angels' trumps alarum sound.

My soul, with Christ join thou in fight ;
Stick to the tents which he hath pight ;
Within his crib is surest ward,
This little Babe will be thy guard ;
If thou wilt foil thy foes with joy,
Then flit not from this heavenly boy.

XI.

THE BURNING BABE.

A S I in hoary winter's night
    Stood shivering in the snow,
Surprised I was with sudden heat,
   Which made my heart to glow ;
And lifting up a fearful eye
   To view what fire was near,
A pretty babe all burning bright,
   Did in the air appear ;

Who scorched with excessive heat,
  Such floods of tears did shed,
As though his floods should quench his flames,
  Which with his tears were bred.
' Alas ! ' quoth he, ' but newly born,
  In fiery heats I fry,
Yet none approach to warm their hearts
  Or feel my fire, but I ;

My faultless breast the furnace is,
  The fuel, wounding thorns ;
Love is the fire, and sighs the smoke,
  The ashes, shames and scorns ;
The fuel justice layeth on,
  And mercy blows the coals,
The metal in this furnace wrought
  Are men's defiled souls :
For which, as now on fire I am,
  To work them to their good,
So will I melt into a bath,
  To wash them in my blood ! '
With this he vanished out of sight,
  And swiftly shrunk away,
And straight I called unto my mind
  That it was Christmas Day.

XII.

THE VIRGIN MARY TO CHRIST ON THE CROSS.

WHAT mist hath dimmed that glorious face? what
seas of grief my sun doth toss?
The golden rays of heavenly grace lie now eclipsed on the
cross.

Jesus! my Love, my Son, my God, behold thy mother
washed in tears :
Thy bloody wounds be made a rod to chasten these my
latter years.

You cruel Jews, come work your ire, upon this worthless
flesh of mine :
And kindle not eternal fire, by wounding him which is
divine.

Thou messenger that didst impart his first descent into
my womb,
Come help me now to cleave my heart, that there I may
my Son entomb.

You angels all, that present were, to show his birth with
harmony ;
Why are you not now ready here, to make a mourning
symphony?

The cause I know, you wail alone and shed your tears in
    secrecy,
Lest I should moved be to moan, by force of heavy
    company.

But wail my soul, thy comfort dies; my woeful womb,
    lament thy fruit;
My heart, give tears unto my eyes, let sorrow string my
    heavy lute.

XIII.

SIR HENRY WOTTON,
1568—1639.

A HYMN TO MY GOD IN A NIGHT OF MY LATE SICKNESS.

O thou great Power, in whom I move,
   For whom I live, to whom I die !
Behold me through thy beams of love,
   Whilst on this couch of tears I lie,
And cleanse my sordid soul within
By thy Christ's blood, the bath of sin.

No hallowed oils, no grains I need,
   No rags of saints, no purging fire ;
One rosy drop from David's seed
   Was worlds of seas to quench thine ire :
O precious ransom ! which once paid,
That *consummatum est* was said ;

And said by him that said no more,
   But sealed it with his sacred breath :
Thou, then, that hast dispunged my score,
   And dying wast the death of Death,
Be to me now, on thee I call,
My life, my strength, my joy, my all !

XIV.

A HYMN.

ETERNAL Mover, whose diffused glory,
To show our grovelling reason what thou art,
Unfolds itself in clouds of nature's story,
Where man, thy proudest creature, acts his part,
Whom yet, alas! I know not why, we call
The world's contracted sum, the little all;

For what are we but lumps of walking clay?
Why should we swell? whence should our spirits rise?
Are not brute beasts as strong, and birds as gay,
Trees longer lived, and creeping things as wise?
Only our souls was left an inward light,
To feel our weakness, and confess thy might.

Thou, then, our strength, father of life and death,
To whom our thanks, our vows, ourselves we owe,
From me, thy tenant of this fading breath,
Accept those lines which from thy goodness flow;
And thou, that wert thy regal prophet's muse,
Do not thy praise in weaker strains refuse.

Let these poor notes ascend unto thy throne,
Where majesty doth sit, with mercy crowned,

Where my Redeemer lives, in whom alone
 The errors of my wandering life are drowned,
Where all the choir of heaven resound the same,
That only thine, thine is the saving name.

Well then, my soul, joy in the midst of pain ;
 Thy Christ, that conquered hell, shall from above
With greater triumph yet return again,
 And conquer his own justice with his love,
Commanding earth and seas to render those
Unto his bliss, for whom he paid his woes.

Now have I done, now are my thoughts at peace,
 And now my joys are stronger than my grief ;
I feel those comforts that shall never cease,
 Future in hope, but present in belief :
Thy words are true, thy promises are just,
And thou wilt find thy dearly-bought in dust.

XV.

JOHN DONNE,
1573—1631.

A HYMN TO CHRIST, AT THE AUTHOR'S LAST GOING INTO GERMANY.

IN what torn ship soever I embark,
  That ship shall be my emblem of thy ark ;
What sea soever swallow me, that flood
Shall be to me an emblem of thy blood.
Though thou with clouds of anger do disguise
Thy face, yet through that mask I know those eyes,
Which, though they turn away sometimes, they never will
    despise.

I sacrifice this island unto thee,
And all whom I love here, and who love me ;
When I have put our seas 'twixt them and me,
Put thou thy sea betwixt my sins and thee.
As the tree's sap doth seek the root below
In winter, in my winter now I go
Where none but thee, the eternal root of true love, I may
    know.

Nor thou, nor thy religion, dost control
The amorousness of an harmonious soul ;

But thou would'st have that love thyself : as thou
Art jealous, Lord, so I am jealous now.
Thou lovest not, till from loving more thou free
My soul : whoever gives, takes liberty :
O, if thou carest not whom I love, alas, thou lovest not
    me !

Seal then this bill of my divorce to all
On whom those fainter beams of love did fall ;   ·
Marry those loves, which in youth scattered be
On fame, wit, hopes—false mistresses—to thee.
Churches are best for prayer that have least light ;
To see God only, I go out of sight :
And to 'scape stormy days, I choose an everlasting night.

XVI.

A HYMN TO GOD THE FATHER.

WILT thou forgive that sin where I begun,
    Which was my sin, though it were done before ?
Wilt thou forgive that sin, through which I run
    And do run still, though still I do deplore?
When thou hast done, thou hast not done ;
      For I have more.

Wilt thou forgive that sin which I have won
   Others to sin, and made my sins their door?
Wilt thou forgive that sin which I did shun
   A year or two, but wallowed in, a score?
When thou hast done, thou hast not done ;
       For I have more.

I have a sin of fear, that when I have spun
   My last thread, I shall perish on the shore ;
But swear by thyself, that at my death thy Son
   Shall shine, as he shines now and heretofore :
And having done that, thou hast done ;
       I fear no more.

XVII.

HYMN TO GOD, MY GOD, IN MY SICKNESS.

SINCE I am coming to that holy room
   Where with the choir of saints for evermore
I shall be made thy music ; as I come,
   I tune the instrument here at the door,
   And what I must do then, think here before.

Whilst my physicians by their love are grown
   Cosmographers, and I their map, who lie
Flat on this bed, that by them may be shown

That this is my south-west discovery
Per fretum febris, by these straits to die.

I joy, that in these straits I see my West ;
    For though these currents yield return to none,
What shall my West hurt me ?   As West and East
    In all flat maps, and I am one, are one,
    So death doth touch the Resurrection.

Is the Pacific Sea my home ?   Or are
    The Eastern riches ?   Is Jerusalem ?
Anyan, and Magellan, and Gibraltar are
    All straits, and none but straits are ways to them,
    Whether where Japhet dwelt, or Cham, or Sem.

We think that Paradise and Calvary,
    Christ's cross and Adam's tree, stood in one place ;
Look, Lord, and find both Adams met in me ;
    As the first Adam's sweat surrounds my face,
    May the last Adam's blood my soul embrace !

So in his purple wrapped receive me, Lord,
    By these his thorns give me his other crown ;
And as to others' souls I preached thy word,
    Be this my text, my sermon to mine own,—
    ' Therefore, that he may raise, the Lord throws down.

XVIII.

BEN JONSON,
1573—1637.

TO THE HOLY TRINITY.

O HOLY, blessed, glorious Trinity
  Of persons, still one God in Unity,
The faithful man's believed mystery,
    Help, help to lift
Myself up to thee, harrowed, torn, and bruised,
By sin and Satan ; and my flesh misused,
As my heart lies in pieces, all confused,
    O take my gift.

All gracious God, the sinners' sacrifice,
A broken heart thou wert not wont despise ;
But 'bove the fat of rams, or bulls, to prize
    An offering meet
For thy acceptance : O behold me right,
And take compassion on my grievous plight !
What odour can be, than a heart contrite,
    To thee more sweet ?

Eternal Father, God who didst create
This all of nothing, gavest it form and fate,
And breathest into it life and light, with state
    To worship thee ;

Eternal God the Son, who not deniedst
To take our nature ; becamest man and diedst,
To pay our debts, upon thy cross, and criedst
            ' All's done in me.'

Eternal Spirit, God from both proceeding,
Father and Son ; the Comforter, in breeding
Pure thoughts in man : with fiery zeal them feeding
            For acts of grace :
Increase these acts, O glorious Trinity
Of persons, still one God in Unity;
Till I attain the longed for mystery
            Of seeing your face,

Beholding one in three, and three in one,
A Trinity, to shine in Union ;
The gladdest light dark man can think upon ;
            O grant it me !
Father, and Son, and Holy Ghost, you three,
All co-eternal in your majesty,
Distinct in persons, yet in Unity
            One God to see.

My Maker, Saviour, and my Sanctifier !
To hear, to meditate, sweeten my desire
With grace, with love, with cherishing entire :
            O, then how blest !

Among thy saints elected to abide,
And with thy angels placed, side by side,
But in thy presence, truly glorified
    Shall I then rest !

XIX.

A HYMN ON THE NATIVITY OF MY SAVIOUR.

I SING the birth was born to-night,
  The author both of life and light ;
    The angels so did sound it.
And like the ravished shepherds said,
Who saw the light, and were afraid,
    Yet searched, and true they found it.

The Son of God, the Eternal King,
That did us all salvation bring,
    And freed the world from danger ;
He whom the whole world could not take,
The Word, which heaven and earth did make,
    Was now laid in a manger.

The Father's wisdom willed it so,
The Son's obedience knew no No,
    Both wills were in one stature ;

And as that wisdom had decreed,
The Word was now made flesh indeed,
    And took on him our nature.

What comfort by him do we win,
Who made himself the price of sin,
    To make us heirs of glory!
To see this Babe, all innocence,
A martyr born in our defence ;
    Can man forget this story ?

XX.

HYMN TO GOD THE FATHER.

H EAR me, O God !
        A broken heart
    Is my best part :
    Use still thy rod,
        That I may prove
        Therein thy love.

    If thou hadst not
        Been stern to me,
        But left me free,

I had forgot
   Myself and thee,

For sin 's so sweet,
   As minds ill bent
   Rarely repent,
Until they meet
   Their punishment.

Who more can crave
   Than thou hast done?
   That gavest a son
To free a slave :
   First made of nought ;
   Withal since bought.

Sin, death, and hell,
   His glorious name
   Quite overcame ;
Yet I rebel,
   And slight the same.

But I'll come in
   Before my loss
   Me further toss,
As sure to win
   Under his cross.

D

PHINEAS FLETCHER,
1581—1650.

XXI.

A HYMN.

DROP, drop, slow tears,
    And bathe those beauteous feet,
Which brought from heaven
    The news and Prince of peace :
Cease not, wet eyes,
    His mercies to entreat ;
To cry for vengeance
    Sin doth never cease :
In your deep floods
    Drown all my faults and fears ;
Nor let his eye
    See sin, but through my tears.

XXII.

PSALM CXXX.

FROM the deeps of grief and fear,
    O Lord, to thee my soul repairs :

From thy heaven bow down thine ear ;
Let thy mercy meet my prayers.
    O if thou mark'st
        What 's done amiss,
    What soul so pure,
        Can see thy bliss?

But with thee sweet mercy stands,
Sealing pardons, working fear :
Wait my soul, wait on his hands ;
Wait mine eye, O wait mine ear :
    If he his eye
        Or tongue affords,
    Watch all his looks.
        Catch all his words.

As a watchman waits for day,
And looks for light, and looks again ;
When the night grows old and gray,
To be relieved he calls amain :
    So look, so wait,
        So long mine eyes,
    To see my Lord,
        My Sun, arise.

Wait ye saints, wait on our Lord ;
For from his tongue sweet mercy flows :

Wait on his Cross, wait on his Word ;
Upon that tree redemption grows.
He will redeem
His Israel
From sin and wrath,
From death and hell.

WILLIAM DRUMMOND,
XXIII.　　　　　　　　　　　　　　1585—1649.

FAITH ABOVE REASON.

S OUL, whom hell did once enthrall,
　　He, he for thine offence
Did suffer death, who could not die at all.
　　O sovereign excellence !
O life of all that lives !
Eternal bounty which each good thing gives!
　　How could death mount so high ?
No wit this point can reach,
Faith only us doth teach,
　　He died for us at all who could not die.

XXIV.   ANON.
                                ? 1588.
     *From William Byrd's " Psalms, Sonnets,
                and Songs."*

I F that a sinner's sighs be angels' food,
     Or that repentant tears be angels' wine,
Accept, O Lord, in this most pensive mood
     These hearty sighs and faithful tears of mine :
That went with Peter forth most sinfully,
But not with Peter wept most bitterly.

If I had David's crown to me betide,
     Or all his purple robes that he did wear,
I would lay then such honour all aside,
     And only seek a sackcloth weed to bear :
His palace would I leave that I might show,
And mourn in cell for such offence, my woe.

There should these hands beat on my pensive breast,
     And sad to death, for sorrow rend my hair,
My voice to call on thee, should never rest,
     Whose grace I seek, whose judgment I do fear :
Upon the ground all grovelling on my face
I would beseech thy favour and good grace.

But since I have not means to make the show
  Of my repentant mind, and yet I see
My sin to greater heap than Peter's grow,
  Whereby the danger more it is to me,
I put my trust in his most precious blood,
Whose life was paid to purchase all our good.

Thy mercy greater is than any sin,
  Thy greatness none can ever comprehend :
Wherefore, O Lord, let me thy mercy win,
  Whose glorious name no time can ever end :
Wherefore I say all praise belongs to thee,
Whom I beseech be merciful to me.

GEORGE WITHER,
1588—1667.

XXV.

A ROCKING HYMN.

SWEET baby, sleep : what ails my dear?
  What ails my darling thus to cry?
Be still, my child, and lend thy ear
  To hear me sing thy lullaby.
My pretty lamb, forbear to weep,
Be still, my dear ; sweet baby, sleep.

Thou blessed soul, what canst thou fear?
  What thing to thee can mischief do?
Thy God is now thy father dear ;
  His holy spouse, thy mother too.
Sweet baby, then, forbear to weep ;
Be still, my babe ; sweet baby, sleep.

Though thy conception was in sin,
  A sacred bathing thou hast had ;
And though thy birth unclean hath been,
  A blameless babe thou now art made.
Sweet baby, then, forbear to weep ;
Be still, my dear ; sweet baby, sleep.

While thus thy lullaby I sing
   For thee great blessings ripening be :
Thine eldest brother is a king,
   And hath a kingdom bought for thee.
Sweet baby, then, forbear to weep ;
Be still, my babe ; sweet baby, sleep.

Sweet baby, sleep, and nothing fear ;
   For, whosoever thee offends,
By thy protector threatened are,
   And God and angels are thy friends.
Sweet baby, then, forbear to weep ;
Be still, my babe ; sweet baby, sleep.

When God with us was dwelling here,
   In little babes he took delight.
Such innocents as thou, my dear,
   Are ever precious in his sight.
Sweet baby, then, forbear to weep ;
Be still, my babe ; sweet baby, sleep.

A little infant once was he,
   And strength, in weakness, then was laid
Upon his virgin mother's knee,
   That power to thee might be conveyed.
Sweet baby, then, forbear to weep ;
Be still, my babe ; sweet baby, sleep.

The King of Kings, when he was born,
  Had not so much for outward ease ;
By him such dressings were not worn ;
  Nor such like swaddling clothes as these.
Sweet baby, then, forbear to weep ;
Be still, my babe ; sweet baby, sleep.

Within a manger lodged thy Lord,
  Where oxen lay, and asses fed ;
Warm rooms we do to thee afford,
  An easy cradle or a bed.
Sweet baby, then, forbear to weep ;
Be still, my babe ; sweet baby, sleep.

The wants, that he did then sustain,
  Have purchased wealth, my babe, for thee ;
And by his torments, and his pain
  Thy rest and ease secured be.
My baby, then, forbear to weep ;
Be still, my babe ; sweet baby, sleep.

Thou hast yet more to perfect this,
  A promise, and an earnest got
Of gaining everlasting bliss,
  Though thou, my babe, receivest it not.
Sweet baby, then, forbear to weep ;
Be still, my babe ; sweet baby, sleep.

XXVI.

INVITATION TO PRAISE.

COME, O come in pious lays,
  Sound we God Almighty's praise ;
Hither bring, in one consent,
Heart and voice and instrument.
Music add of every kind,
Sound the trump, the cornet wind ;
Strike the viol, touch the lute ;
Let no tongue nor string be mute,
Nor a creature dumb be found,
That hath either voice or sound.

Let those things which do not live,
In still music praises give ;
Lowly pipe, ye worms that creep,
On the earth, or in the deep ;
Loud aloft your voices strain,
Beasts and monsters of the main ;
Birds, your warbling treble sing ;
Clouds, your peals of thunders ring ;
Sun and moon, exalted higher,
And bright stars, augment the choir.

Come, ye sons of human race,
In this chorus take your place ;
And, amid the mortal throng,
Be you masters of the song.
Angels and supernal powers,
Be the noblest tenor yours ;
Let in praise of God the sound
Run a never-ending round,
That our song of praise may be
Everlasting as is he.

From earth's vast and hollow womb,
Music's deepest bass may come ;
Seas and floods, from shore to shore,
Shall their counter-tenors roar.
To this concert, when we sing,
Whistling winds, your descants bring ;
That our song may over-climb
All the bounds of place and time,
And ascend, from sphere to sphere,
To the great Almighty's ear.

So, from heaven, on earth he shall
Let his gracious blessings fall ;
And this huge wide orb we see
Shall one choir, one temple be ;

Where, in such a praiseful tone
We will sing what he hath done,
That the cursed fiends below
Shall thereat impatient grow.
Then, O come, in pious lays,
Sound we God Almighty's praise.

ROBERT HERRICK,
1591—1674.

XXVII.

TO KEEP A TRUE LENT.

I S this a fast, to keep
    The larder lean?
        And clean
From fat of veals, and sheep?

Is it to quit the dish
    Of flesh, yet still
        To fill
The platter high with fish?

Is it to fast an hour,
    Or ragged to go,
        Or show
A downcast look, and sour?

No : 'tis a fast, to dole
    Thy sheaf of wheat,
        And meat,
Unto the hungry soul.

It is to fast from strife,
From old debate,
And hate ;
To circumcise thy life.

To show a heart grief-rent ;
To starve thy sin,
Not bin ;
And that's to keep thy Lent.

XXVIII.

TO DEATH.

THOU bidst me come away,
And I'll no longer stay,
Than for to shed some tears
For faults of former years ;
And to repent some crimes,
Done in the present times :
And next, to take a bit
Of Bread, and Wine with it :
To don my robes of love,
Fit for the place above ;
To gird my loins about
With charity throughout ;

And so to travel hence
With feet of innocence :
These done, I'll only cry
God mercy ; and so die.

XXIX.

AN ODE OF THE BIRTH OF OUR SAVIOUR.

IN numbers, and but these few,
    I sing thy birth, O Jesu !
Thou pretty baby, born here,
With superabundant scorn here :
Who for thy princely port here,
        Hadst for thy place
        Of birth, a base
Out-stable for thy court here.

Instead of neat inclosures
Of interwoven osiers ;
Instead of fragrant posies
Of daffodils, and roses ;
Thy cradle, kingly stranger,
        As gospel tells,
        Was nothing else,
But, here, a homely manger.

But we with silks, not crewels,
With sundry precious jewels,
And lily-work will dress thee ;
And as we dispossess thee
Of clouts, we'll make a chamber,
   Sweet Babe, for thee,
   Of ivory,
And plastered round with amber.

The Jews they did disdain thee,
But we will entertain thee
With glories to await here
Upon thy princely state here,
And more for love, than pity.
   From year to year
   We'll make thee, here,
A free-born of our city.

XXX

HIS LITANY, TO THE HOLY SPIRIT.

IN the hour of my distress,
 When temptations me oppress,
And when I my sins confess,
   Sweet Spirit comfort me !

E

When I lie within my bed,
Sick in heart and sick in head,
And with doubts discomforted,
      Sweet Spirit comfort me !

When the house doth sigh and weep,
And the world is drowned in sleep,
Yet mine eyes the watch do keep ;
      Sweet Spirit comfort me !

When the artless doctor sees
No one hope, but of his fees,
And his skill runs on the lees ;
      Sweet Spirit comfort me !

When his potion and his pill,
Has, or none, or little skill,
Meet for nothing, but to kill,
      Sweet Spirit comfort me !

When the passing-bell doth toll,
And the furies in a shoal
Come to fright a parting soul ;
      Sweet Spirit comfort me !

When the tapers now burn blue,
And the comforters are few,

And that number more than true ;
  Sweet Spirit comfort me !

When the priest his last hath prayed,
And I nod to what is said,
'Cause my speech is now decayed ;
  Sweet Spirit comfort me !

When, God knows, I'm tossed about,
Either with despair, or doubt ;
Yet before the glass be out,
  Sweet Spirit comfort me !

When the Tempter me pursueth
With the sins of all my youth,
And half damns me with untruth ;
  Sweet Spirit comfort me !

When the flames and hellish cries
Fright mine ears, and fright mine eyes,
And all terrors me surprise ;
  Sweet Spirit comfort me !

When the Judgment is revealed,
And that opened which was sealed,
When to thee I have appealed ;
  Sweet Spirit comfort me !

XXXI.

FRANCIS QUARLES,
1592—1644.

ALL IS VANITY AND VEXATION
OF SPIRIT.

HOW is the anxious soul of man befooled
  In his desire,
That thinks an hectic fever can be cooled
  In flames of fire ;
Or hopes to rake full heaps of burnished gold
  From nasty mire !
A whining lover may as well request
  A scornful breast
To melt in gentle tears, as woo the world for rest.

Let wit and all her studied plots effect
  The best they can ;
Let smiling fortune prosper and perfect
  What wit began ;
Let earth advise with both, and so project
  A happy man ;
Let wit or fawning fortune vie their best ;
  He may be blest
With all that earth can give : but earth can give no rest.

Whose gold is double with a careful hand,
    His cares are double,
The pleasure, honour, wealth of sea and land
    Bring but a trouble ;
The world itself, and all the world's command,
    Is but a bubble.
The strong desires of man's insatiate breast
    May stand possessed
Of all that earth can give ; but earth can give no rest.

The world's a seeming Paradise, but her own
    And man's tormentor ;
Appearing fixed, yet but a rolling stone
    Without a tenter ;
It is a vast circumference, where none
    Can find a centre.
Of more than earth, can earth make none possessed ;
    And he that least
Regards this restless world, shall in this world find rest.

True rest consists not in the oft revying
    Of worldly dross ;
Earth's miry purchase is not worth the buying ;
    Her gain is loss ;
Her rest but giddy toil, if not relying
    Upon her cross.

How worldlings droyl for trouble !   That fond breast
    That is possessed
Of earth without a cross has earth without a rest.

XXXII.

WHOM HAVE I IN HEAVEN BUT THEE? AND WHAT DESIRE I ON EARTH IN RESPECT OF THEE?

I LOVE, and have some cause to love, the earth :
  She is my Maker's creature, therefore good :
She is my mother, for she gave me birth ;
She is my tender nurse ; she gives me food :
    But what's a creature, Lord, compared with thee ?
    Or what's my mother, or my nurse to me ?

I love the air : her dainty sweets refresh
My drooping soul, and to new sweets invite me ;
Her shrill-mouthed choir sustain me with their flesh,
And with their Polyphonian notes delight me :
    But what's the air or all the sweets that she
    Can bless my soul withal, compared to thee ?

I love the sea : she is my fellow-creature ;
My careful purveyor ; she provides me store :

She walls me round ; she makes my diet greater ;
She wafts my treasure from a foreign shore ;
  But Lord of oceans, when compared with thee,
  What is the ocean, or her wealth to me ?

To heaven's high city I direct my journey,
Whose spangled suburbs entertain mine eye ;
Mine eye, by contemplation's great attorney,
Transcends the crystal pavement of the sky :
  But what is heaven, great God, compared to thee ?
  Without thy presence heaven 's no heaven to me.

Without thy presence earth gives no refection ;
Without thy presence sea affords no treasure ;
Without thy presence air 's a rank infection ;
Without thy presence heaven itself's no pleasure :
  If not possest, if not enjoyed in thee,
  What's earth, or sea, or air, or heaven to me ?

The highest honours that the world can boast
Are subjects far too low for my desire ;
The brightest beams of glory are, at most,
But dying sparkles of thy living fire :
  The proudest flames that earth can kindle, be
  But nightly glow-worms, if compared to thee.

Without thy presence wealth are bags of cares ;
Wisdom, but folly; joy, disquiet sadness ;

Friendship is treason, and delights are snares;
Pleasures but pain, and mirth but pleasing madness:
    Without thee, Lord, things be not what they be,
    Nor have they being, when compared with thee.

In having all things, and not thee, what have I?
Not having thee, what have my labours got?
Let me enjoy but thee, what further crave I?
And having thee alone, what have I not?
    I wish nor sea, nor land, nor would I be
    Possest of heaven, heaven unpossest of thee.

XXXIII.

YET A LITTLE WHILE IS THE LIGHT WITH YOU.

THE day grows old, the low-pitched lamp hath made
        No less than treble shade,
And the descending damp doth now prepare
        To uncurl bright Titan's hair;
Whose western wardrobe now begins to unfold
        Her purples, tinged with gold,
To clothe his evening glory, when the alarms
        Of rest shall call to rest in restless Thetis' arms.

Nature now calls to supper, to refresh
    The spirits of all flesh ;
The toiling ploughman drives his thirsty teams
    To taste the slippery streams ;
The droyling swine-herd knocks away, and feasts
    His hungry whining guests ;
The boxbill ouzel, and the dappled thrush
Like hungry rivals meet at their beloved bush.

And now the cold autumnal dews are seen
    To cobweb every green ;
And by the low-shorn rowans doth appear
    The fast-declining year ;
The sapless branches doff their summer suits,
    And wain their winter fruits ;
And stormy blasts have forced the quaking trees
To wrap their trembling limbs in suits of mossy frieze.

Our wasted taper now hath brought her light
    To the next door to-night ;
Her sprightless flame grown with great snuff, doth turn
    Sad as her neighbouring urn ;
Her slender inch, that yet unspent remains,
    Lights but to further pains,
And in a silent language bids her guest
Prepare his weary limbs to take eternal rest.

Now careful age hath pitched her painful plough
    Upon the furrowed brow ;
And snowy blasts of discontented care
    Have blanched the falling hair ;
Suspicious envy mixed with jealous spite
    Disturbs his weary night ;
He threatens youth with age ; and now, alas !
He owns not what he is, but vaunts the man he was.

Grey hairs, peruse thy days, and let thy past
    Read lectures to thy last :
Those hasty wings that hurried them away
    Will give these days no day:
The constant wheels of Nature scorn to tire
    Until her works expire :
That blast that nipped thy youth, will ruin thee ;
The hand that shook the branch will quickly strike the tree.

GEORGE HERBERT,
1593—1633.

XXXIV.

EASTER DAY.

I GOT me flowers to strew thy way,
　I got me boughs off many a tree ;
But thou wast up by break of day,
　And brought'st thy sweets along with thee.

The sun arising in the East
　Though he give light, and the East perfume,
If they should offer to contest
　With thy arising, they presume.

Can there be any day but this,
　Though many suns to shine endeavour ?
We count three hundred, but we miss :
　There is but one, and that one ever.

XXXV.

CHRISTMAS.

THE shepherds sing ; and shall I silent be ?
      My God, no hymn for thee ?
My soul 's a shepherd too ; a flock it feeds
      Of thoughts and words and deeds :
The pasture is thy word ; the streams thy grace,
      Enriching all the place.

Shepherd and flock shall sing, and all my powers
      Out-sing the daylight hours ;
Then we will chide the sun for letting night
      Take up his place and right :
We sing one common Lord ; wherefore he should
      Himself the candle hold.

I will go searching till I find a sun
      Shall stay till we have done ;
A willing shiner, that shall shine as gladly
      As frost-nipped suns look sadly :
Then we will sing, and shine all our own day,
      And one another pay :

His beams shall cheer my breast, and both so twine,
      Till ev'n his beams sing, and my music shine.

XXXVI.

DIALOGUE.

SWEETEST Saviour, if my soul
    Were but worth the having,
Quickly should I then control
    Any thought of waving.
But when all my care and pains
Cannot give the name of gains
To thy wretch so full of stains,
What delight or hope remains?

What, child, is the balance thine;
    Thine the poise and measure?
If I say thou shalt be mine
    Finger not my treasure.
What the gains in having thee
Do amount to, only he
Who for man was sold can see;
That transferred the accounts to me.

But as I can see no merit
    Leading to this favour,

So the way to fit me for it
  Is beyond my savour.
As the reason, then, is thine,
So the way is none of mine,
I disclaim the whole design ;
Sin disclaims and I resign.

That is all :—if that I could
  Get without repining ;
And my clay, my creature, would
  Follow my resigning ;
That as I did freely part
With my glory and desert,
Left all joys to feel all smart—
Ah ! no more : thou break'st my heart.

XXXVII.

THE SEARCH.

WHITHER, O whither art thou fled,
      My Lord, my Love ?
My searches are my daily bread,
      Yet never prove.

My knees pierce earth, mine eyes the sky ;
      And yet the sphere

And centre both to me deny
    That thou art there.

Yet can I mark how herbs below
    Grow green and gay,
As if to meet thee they did know,
    While I decay.

Yet can I mark how stars above
    Simper and shine,
As having keys unto thy love,
    While poor I pine.

I sent a sigh to seek thee out,
    Deep drawn in pain,
Winged like an arrow, but my scout
    Returns in vain.

I tuned another,—having store,—
    Into a groan,
Because the search was dumb before ;
    But all was one.

Lord, dost thou some new fabric mould
    Which favour wins,
And keeps the present ; leaving the old
    Unto their sins.

Where is my God? what hidden place
    Conceals thee still?
What covert dare eclipse thy face?
    Is it thy will?

O let not that of any thing;
    Let rather brass,
Or steel, or mountains be thy ring,
    And I will pass.

Thy will such an intrenching is
    As passeth thought :
To it all strength, all subtilties
    Are things of nought.

Thy will such a strange distance is
    As that to it
East and West touch, the poles do kiss,
    And parallels meet.

Since then my grief must be as large
    As is thy space,
Thy distance from me ; see my charge,
    Lord, see my case.

O take these bars, these lengths away ;
    Turn, and restore me,
‘ Be not Almighty,’ let me say,
    ‘ Against, but for me.’

GEORGE HERBERT.

When thou dost turn, and wilt be near,
    What edge so keen,
What point so piercing can appear
    To come between?

For as thy absence doth excel
    All distance known,
So doth thy nearness bear the bell,
    Making two one.

SIMON WASTELL
circa 1600.

XXXVIII.

UPON THE IMAGE OF DEATH.

BEFORE my face the picture hangs
   That daily should put me in mind
Of those cold qualms and bitter pangs,
   That shortly I am like to find :
But yet, alas ! full little I
Do think hereon that I must die.

I often look upon the face
   Most ugly, grisly, bare, and thin ;
I often view the hollow place
   Where eyes and nose had sometime been ;
I see the bones, across that lie,
Yet little think that I must die.

I read the label underneath,
   That telleth me whereto I must :
I see the sentence eke that saith
   ' Remember, man, that thou art dust.'
But yet, alas ! but seldom I
Do think indeed that I must die.

Continually at my bed's head
   An hearse doth hang, which doth me tell
That I ere morning may be dead,
   Though now I feel myself full well :
But yet, alas ! for all this I
Have little mind that I must die.

The gown which I do use to wear,
   The knife wherewith I cut my meat,
And eke that old and ancient chair
   Which is my only usual seat,
All these do tell me I must die,
And yet my life amend not I.

My ancestors are turned to clay,
   And many of my mates are gone,
My youngers daily drop away,
   And can I think to 'scape alone ?
No, no, I know that I must die,
And yet my life amend not I.

If none can 'scape death's dreadful dart,
   If rich and poor his beck obey,
If strong, if wise, if all do smart,
   Then I to 'scape shall have no way.
O grant me grace, O God, that I
My life may mend, sith I must die.

WILLIAM HABINGTON.
born 1605.

XXXIX.

NOX NOCTI INDICAT SCIENTIAM.

WHEN I survey the bright
    Celestial sphere,
So rich with jewels hung, that night
Doth like an Æthiop bride appear ;

My soul her wings doth spread
    And heavenward flies,
The Almighty's mysteries to read
In the large volumes of the skies.

For the bright firmament
    Shoots forth no flame
So silent but is eloquent
In speaking the Creator's name.

No unregarded star
    Contracts its light
Into so small a character,
Removed far from our human sight,

But if we steadfast look,
    We shall discern
In it as in some holy book,
How man may heavenly knowledge learn.

    It tells the conqueror,
        That far stretched power
Which his proud dangers traffic for,
Is but the triumph of an hour :

    That from the furthest north,
        Some nation may
Yet undiscovered issue forth
And o'er his new got conquest sway ;

    Some nation yet shut in
        With hills of ice
May be let out to scourge his sin
Till they shall equal him in vice.

    And then they likewise shall
        Their ruin have,
For as yourselves your empires fall,
And every kingdom hath a grave.

    Thus those celestial fires,
        Though seeming mute

The fallacy of our desires
And all the pride of life confute.

For they have watched since first
The world had birth ;
And found sin in itself accursed,
And nothing permanent on earth.

XL.

THOMAS WASHBOURNE,
1606—1687.

GOD'S TWO DWELLINGS.

L ORD ! thou hast told us that there be
Two dwellings which belong to thee,
And those two, that's the wonder,
Are far asunder.

The one the highest heaven is,
The mansions of eternal bliss;
The other's the contrite
And humble sprite.

Not like the princes of the earth,
Who think it much below their birth
To come within the door
Of people poor.

No, such is thy humility,
That though thy dwelling be on high,
Thou dost thyself abase
To the lowest place.

Where'er thou seest a sinful soul
Deploring his offences foul,
 To him thou wilt descend,
 And be his friend.

Thou wilt come in, and with him sup,
And from a low state raise him up,
 Till thou hast made him eat
 Blest angel's meat.

Thus thou wilt him with honour crown
Who in himself is first cast down,
 And humbled for his sins,
 That thy love wins.

Though heaven be high, the gate is low,
And he that comes in there must bow :
 The lofty looks shall ne'er
 Have entrance there.

O God ! since thou delight'st to rest
In the humble contrite breast
 First make me so to be,
 Then dwell with me.

JOHN MILTON,
1608—1674.

XLI.

UPON THE CIRCUMCISION.

YE flaming powers, and winged warriors bright,
That erst with music and triumphant song,
First heard by happy watchful shepherds' ear,
So sweetly sung your joy the clouds along,
Through the soft silence of the listening night,
Now mourn; and, if sad share with us to bear
Your fiery essence can distil no tear,
Burn in your sighs, and borrow
Seas wept from our deep sorrow.
He who with all heaven's heraldry whilere
Entered the world now bleeds to give us ease.
Alas! how soon our sin
  Sore doth begin
    His infancy to seize.

O more exceeding love, or law more just?
Just law, indeed, but more exceeding love!
For we, by rightful doom remediless,
Were lost in death, till he, that dwelt above
High-throned in secret bliss, for us frail dust
Emptied his glory, even to nakedness;

And that great covenant which we still transgress
Entirely satisfied ;
And the full wrath beside
Of vengeful justice bore for our excess ;
And seals obedience first, with wounding smart,
This day ; but O ! ere long,
   Huge pangs and strong
     Will pierce more near his heart.

XLII.

ON TIME.

FLY, envious Time, till thou run out thy race :
   Call on the lazy leaden-stepping Hours,
Whose speed is but the heavy plummet's pace ;
And glut thyself with what thy womb devours,
Which is no more than what is false and vain,
And merely mortal dross ;
So little is our loss,
So little is thy gain !
For, whenas each thing bad thou hast entombed,
And, last of all, thy greedy self consumed,
Then long eternity shall greet our bliss
With an individual kiss,
And joy shall overtake us as a flood ;

When every thing that is sincerely good
And perfectly divine,
With Truth, and Peace, and Love, shall ever shine
About the supreme throne
Of him, to whose happy-making sight alone
When once our heavenly-guided soul shall climb,
Then, all this earthy grossness quit,
Attired with stars we shall for ever sit,
Triumphing over Death, and Chance, and thee, O Time !

XLIII.

AT A SOLEMN MUSIC.

BLEST pair of sirens, pledges of heaven's joy,
Sphere-born harmonious sisters, Voice and Verse,
Wed your divine sounds, and mixed power employ,
Dead things with inbreathed sense able to pierce ;
And to our high-raised phantasy present
That undisturbed song of pure concent,
Aye sung before the sapphire-coloured throne
To him that sits thereon,
With saintly shout and solemn jubilee ;
Where the bright seraphim in burning row
Their loud uplifted angel-trumpets blow ;
And the cherubic host, in thousand quires,

Touch their immortal harps of golden wires,
With those just spirits that wear victorious palms,
Hymns devout and holy psalms
Singing everlastingly :
That we on earth, with undiscording voice,
May rightly answer that melodious noise ;
As once we did, till disproportioned sin
Jarred against nature's chime, and with harsh din
Broke the fair music that all creatures made
To their great Lord, whose love their motion swayed
In perfect diapason, whilst they stood
In first obedience, and their state of good.
O ! may we soon again renew that song,
And keep in tune with heaven, till God ere long
To his celestial consort us unite,
To live with him, and sing in endless morn of light.

XLIV.

RICHARD CRASHAW,
1612—1649.

UPON THE BLEEDING CRUCIFIX.

JESU, no more ! It is full tide :
　From thy head and from thy feet,
From thy hands and from thy side
　All the purple rivers meet.

What need thy fair head bear a part
　In showers, as if thine eyes had none ?
What need they help to drown thy heart,
　That strives in torrents of its own ?

Watered by the showers they bring,
　The thorns that thy blest brow encloses,
A cruel and a costly spring,
　Conceive proud hopes of proving roses.

Thy restless feet now cannot go
　For us and our eternal good,
As they were ever wont.　What though ?
　They swim, alas ! in their own flood.

Thy hand to give thou canst not lift ;
  Yet will thy hand still giving be.
It gives, but O itself's the gift :
  It gives though bound ; though bound 'tis free.

But O thy side, thy deep-digged side !
  That hath a double Nilus going :
Nor ever was the Pharian tide
  Half so fruitful, half so flowing.

No hair so small, but pays his river
  To this Red Sea of thy blood ;
Their little channels can deliver
  Something to the general flood.

But while I speak, whither are ye run
  All the rivers named before ?
I counted wrong, there is but one ;
  But O that one is one all o'er.

Rain-swoln rivers may rise proud,
  Bent all to drown and overflow ;
But when indeed all's overflowed,
  They themselves are drowned too.

This, thy blood's deluge, a dire chance
  Dear Lord to thee, to us is found

A deluge of deliverance ;
A deluge lest we should be drowned.
Ne'er wast thou in a sense so sadly true,
The well of living waters, Lord, till now.

XLV.

CHRIST'S VICTORY.

CHRIST, when he died,
   Deceived the cross,
And on death's side
   Threw all the loss :
The captive world awaked and found
The prisoners loose, the jailor bound.

O dear and sweet dispute
'Twixt death's and love's far different fruit,
   Different as far
   As antidotes and poisons are :
By the first fatal tree
Both life and liberty
   Were sold and slain ;
   By this they both look up and live again.

O strange mysterious strife,
Of open death and hidden life !
When on the cross my King did bleed,
Life seemed to die, death died indeed.

JEREMY TAYLOR,
1613—1667.

XLVI.

CHRIST'S COMING TO JERUSALEM IN TRIUMPH.

L ORD come away,
Why dost thou stay?
Thy road is ready ; and thy paths, made strait,
    With longing expectation, wait
    The consecration of thy beauteous feet.
Ride on triumphantly ; behold we lay
Our lusts and proud wills in thy way.
Hosanna ! welcome to our hearts ! Lord, here
Thou hast a temple too, and full as dear
As that of Sion ; and as full of sin :
Nothing but thieves and robbers dwell therein :
Enter, and chase them forth, and cleanse the floor ;
Crucify them, that they may never more
    Profane that holy place
    Where thou hast chose to set thy face,
And then if our stiff tongues shall be
Mute in the praises of thy deity,
    The stones out of the temple-wall
    Shall cry aloud and call
Hosanna ! and thy glorious footsteps greet.

G

XLVII.

A PRAYER.

M Y soul doth pant towards thee
     My God, source of eternal life :
Flesh fights with me,
O ! end the strife
And part us, that in peace I may
                    Unclay

My wearied spirit, and take
My flight to thy eternal spring ;
          Where for his sake
          Who is my king,
I may wash all my tears away
                    That day.

Thou conqueror of death,
Glorious triumpher o'er the grave,
          Whose holy breath
          Was spent to save
Lost mankind ; make me to be styled
                    Thy child,

And take me when I die
And go unto my dust, my soul
>>Above the sky
>>With saints enroll,
That in thine arms for ever I
>>May lie.

XLVIII.

JOHN AUSTIN,
1613—1669.

A HYMN.

DEAR Jesu ! when, when will it be
That I no more shall break with thee ?
When will this war of passions cease,
And let my soul enjoy thy peace ?

Here I repent and sin again :
Now I revive and now am slain ;
Slain with the same unhappy dart,
Which, O ! too often wounds my heart.

When, dearest Lord ! when shall I be
A garden sealed to all but thee ?
No more exposed, no more undone ;
But live and grow to thee alone.

'Tis not, alas ! on this low earth
That such pure flowers can find a birth :
Only they spring above the skies,
Where none can live till here he dies.

Then let me die, that I may go
And dwell where those bright lilies grow ;
Where those blest plants of glory rise,
And make a safer paradise.

No dangerous fruit, no tempting Eve,
No crafty serpent to deceive ;
But we like gods indeed shall be :
O let me die that life to see !

Thus says my song ; but does my heart
Join with the words, and sing its part ?
Am I so thorough wise to choose
The other world and this refuse ?

Why should I not ? what do I find
That fully here contents my mind ?
What is this meat, and drink, and sleep,
That such poor things from heaven should keep ?

What is this honour, or great place,
Or bag of money, or fair face,
What's all the world that thus we should
Still long to dwell with flesh and blood ?

Fear not, my soul ; stand to the word
Which thou hast sung to thy dear Lord :

Let but thy love be firm and true,
And with more heat thy wish renew.

O may this dying life make haste
To die into true life at last :
No hope have I to live before ;
But there to live and die no more.

XLIX.

THE PENITENT'S PRAISE.

L ORD, now the time returns
      For weary men to rest ;
And lay aside those pains and cares
    With which our day 's oppressed,

Or rather change our thoughts
    To more concerning cares,
How to redeem our misspent time,
    With sighs, and tears, and prayers.

How to provide for heaven,
    That place of rest and peace :
Where our full joys shall never wain,
    Our pleasures never cease.

Blest be thy love, dear Lord,
   That taught us this sweet way;
Only to love thee, for thyself,
   And for that love obey.

O thou our soul's chief hope,
   We to thy mercy fly ;
Where'er we are thou canst protect,
   Whate'er we need supply.

Whether we sleep or wake,
   To thee we both resign ;
By thee we see, as well as day
   If thy light on us shine.

Whether we live or die,
   Both we submit to thee ;
In death we live, as well as life,
   If thine in death we be.

                                    ABRAHAM COWLEY,
L.   1618—1667.

CHRIST'S PASSION.

E NOUGH, my muse, of earthly things,
    And inspirations but of wind ;
Take up thy lute, and to it bind
Loud and everlasting strings,
And on them play, and to them sing,
The happy mournful stories,
The lamentable glories
Of the great crucified King !
Mountainous heap of wonders ! which dost rise
    Till earth thou joinest with the skies !
Too large at bottom, and at top too high,
    To be half seen by mortal eye ;
    How shall I grasp this boundless thing ?
    What shall I play ? what shall I sing ?
I'll sing the mighty riddle of mysterious love,
Which neither wretched man below, nor blessed spirits
        above,
    With all their comments can explain,
How all the whole world's life to die did not disdain !

I'll sing the searchless depths of the compassion divine,
 The depths unfathomed yet
 By reason's plummet, and the line of wit ;
 Too light the plummet, and too short the line ;
 How the eternal Father did bestow
His own eternal Son as ransom for his foe ;
 I'll sing aloud that all the world may hear
 The triumph of the buried Conqueror ;
 How hell was by its prisoner captive led,
And the great slayer, Death, slain by the dead.

 Methinks I hear of murdered men the voice
 Mixed with the murderers' confused noise,
  Sound from the top of Calvary ;
 My greedy eyes fly up the hill, and see
Who 'tis hangs there, the midmost of the three ;
  O ! how unlike the others he ;
Look ! how he bends his gentle head with blessings from
   the tree,
 His gracious hands, ne'er stretched but to do good,
  Are nailed to the infamous wood !
  And sinful man does fondly bind
The arms which he extends to embrace all human kind.

  Unhappy man ! canst thou stand by and see
  All this as patiently as he ?
   Since he thy sins doth bear,
  Make thou his sufferings thine own,

And weep, and sigh, and groan,
And beat thy breast, and tear
Thy garments and thy hair,
And let thy grief, and let thy love,
Through all thy bleeding bowels move !
Dost thou not see thy Prince in purple clad all o'er,
Not purple brought from the Sidonian shore,
But made at home with richer gore ?
Dost thou not see the roses which adorn
The thorny garland by him worn ?
Dost thou not see the livid traces
Of the sharp scourges' rude embraces ?
If yet thou feelest not the smart
Of thorns and scourges in thy heart,
If that be yet not crucified,
Look on his hands, look on his feet, look on his side !

Open, Oh ! open wide the fountains of thine eyes,
And let them call
Their stock of moisture forth, where'er it lies ;
For this will ask it all.
'Twould all, alas ! too little be,
Though thy salt tears come from a sea.
Canst thou deny him this, when he
Has opened all his vital springs for thee ?
Take heed, for by his side's mysterious flood
May well be understood
That he will still require some waters to his blood.

LI.

ANDREW MARVELL,
1621—1678.

THE CORONET.

WHEN for the thorns with which I long, too long,
　　With many a piercing wound,
My Saviour's head have crowned,
I seek with garlands to redress that wrong :
Through every garden, every mead,
　　I gather flowers, my fruits are only flowers,
　　Dismantling all the fragrant towers
That once adorned my shepherdess's head :
And now, when I have summed up all my store,
　　Thinking, so I myself deceive,
　　So rich a chaplet thence to weave
As never yet the King of Glory wore :
Alas ! I find the Serpent old,
‘　That, twining in his speckled breast,
About the flowers disguised, does fold
　　With wreaths of fame and interest.

Ah ! foolish man, that would'st debase with them,
And mortal glory, heaven's diadem ;
But thou who only could'st the Serpent tame,
Either his slippery knots at once untie,
And disentangle all his winding snare ;

Or shatter too with him my curious frame,
And let these wither so that he may die—
Though set with skill, and chosen out with care :
That they, while thou on both their spoils dost tread,
May crown thy feet, that could not crown thy head.

LII.

A DIALOGUE BETWEEN THE RESOLVED
SOUL AND CREATED PLEASURE.

COURAGE, my soul, now learn to wield
The weight of thine immortal shield ;
Close on thy head thy helmet bright,
Balance thy sword against the fight ;
See where an army, strong as fair,
With silken banners spread the air !
Now, if thou beest that thing divine,
In this day's combat let it shine ;
And show that Nature wants an art
To conquer one resolved heart.

PLEASURE.

Welcome the creation's guest,
Lord of earth and heaven's heir !

Lay aside that warlike crest,
 And of Nature's banquet share ;
Where the souls of fruits and flowers
Stand prepared to heighten yours.

SOUL.

I sup above, and cannot stay,
To bait so long upon the way.

PLEASURE.

On these downy pillows lie,
Whose soft plumes will thither fly ;
On these roses, strewed so plain
Lest one leaf thy side should strain :

SOUL.

My gentler rest is on a thought—
Conscious of doing what I ought.

PLEASURE.

If thou beest with perfumes pleased,
Such as oft the gods appeased,
Thou in fragrant clouds shalt show,
Like another god below.

SOUL.

A soul that knows not to presume,
Is heaven's, and its own, perfume.

PLEASURE.

Every thing does seem to vie
Which should first attract thine eye,
But since none deserves that grace,
In this crystal view thy face.

SOUL.

When the Creator's skill is prized,
The rest is all but earth disguised.

PLEASURE.

Hark how music then prepares
For thy stay these charming airs,
Which the posting winds recall,
And suspend the river's fall.

SOUL.

Had I but any time to lose,
On this I would it all dispose.
Cease tempter ! None can chain a mind,
Whom this sweet cordage cannot bind.

CHORUS.

Earth cannot show so brave a sight,
  As when a single soul does fence
  The batteries of alluring sense,

And heaven views it with delight.
  Then persevere ; for still new charges sound,
  And if thou overcomest thou shalt be crowned.

PLEASURE.

All that's costly, fair, and sweet,
  Which scatteringly doth shine,
Shall within one beauty meet,
  And she be only thine.

SOUL.

If things of sight such heavens be,
What heavens are those we cannot see ?

PLEASURE.

Wheresoe'er thy foot shall go
  The minted gold shall lie,
Till thou purchase all below,
  And want new worlds to buy.

SOUL.

Wer't not for price who'ld value gold ?
And that's worth naught that can be sold.

PLEASURE.

Wilt thou all the glory have
  That war or peace commend ?
Half the world shall be thy slave,
  The other half thy friend.

SOUL.

What friends, if to myself untrue?
What slaves, unless I captive you?

PLEASURE.

Thou shalt know each hidden cause,
And see the future time ;
Try what depth the centre draws,
And then to heaven climb.

SOUL.

None thither mounts by the degree
Of knowledge, but humility.

CHORUS.

Triumph, triumph, victorious soul !
The world has not one pleasure more :
The rest does lie beyond the pole,
And is thine everlasting store.

LIII.

HENRY VAUGHAN,
1621—1695.

DEATH. A DIALOGUE.

SOUL.

'TIS a sad land, that in one day
   Hath dulled thee thus ; when death shall freeze
Thy blood to ice, and thou must stay
   Tenant for years, and centuries ;
How wilt thou brook 't ?—

BODY.

I cannot tell ;—
But if all sense wings not with thee,
   And something still be left the dead,
I'll wish my curtains off, to free
   Me from so dark, and sad a bed :

A nest of nights, a gloomy sphere,
   Where shadows thicken, and the cloud
Sits on the sun's brow all the year,
   And nothing moves without a shroud.

SOUL.

'Tis so : But as thou sawest that night
   We travelled in, our first attempt

H

Were dull and blind, but custom straight
  Our fears and falls brought to contempt.

Then, when the ghastly twelve was past,
  We breathed still for a blushing east,
And bade the lazy sun make haste,
  And on sure hopes, though long, did feast.

But when we saw the clouds to crack,
  And in those crannies light appeared,
We thought the day then was not slack,
  And pleased ourselves with what we feared.

Just so it is in death.   But thou
  Shalt in thy mother's bosom sleep,
Whilst I each minute groan to know
  How near Redemption creeps.
Then shall we meet to mix again, and met,
'Tis last good night ; our sun shall never set.

LIV.

CORRUPTION.

SURE it was so.   Man in those early days
    Was not all stone, and earth ;
He shined a little, and by those weak rays,
    Had some glimpse of his birth.
He saw heaven o'er his head, and knew from whence
    He came, condemned, hither ;
And, as first love grows strongest, so from hence
    His mind soon progressed thither.
Things here were strange unto him : sweat, and toil ;
    All was a thorn or weed ;
Nor did those last, but, like himself, died still
    As soon as they did seed ;
They seemed to quarrel with him ; for that act
    That fell him, foiled them all ;
He drew the curse upon the world, and cracked
    The whole frame with his fall.
This made him long for home, as loath to stay
    With murmurers, and foes ;
He sighed for Eden, and would often say
    ' Ah ! what bright days were those.'
Nor was heaven cold unto him ; for each day

The valley, or the mountain
Afforded visits, and still Paradise lay
    In some green shade, or fountain.
Angels lay leiger here ; each bush, and cell,
    Each oak, and high-way knew them ;
Walk but the fields, or sit down at some well,
    And he was sure to view them.
Almighty Love ! where art thou now ? mad man
    Sits down, and freezeth on ;
He raves, and swears to stir nor fire, nor fan,
    But bids the thread be spun.
I see thy curtains closely drawn ; thy bow
    Looks dim too in the cloud ;
Sin triumphs still, and man is sunk below
    The centre, and his shroud.
All's in dark sleep, and night : thick darkness lies
    And hatcheth o'er thy people—
But hark ! what trumpet's that ? what angel cries
    ' Arise ! thrust in thy sickle ' ?

LV.

THE KNOT.

BRIGHT Queen of heaven ! God's virgin Spouse !
   The glad world's blessed maid !
Whose beauty tied life to thy house,
   And brought us saving aid.

Thou art the true love's-knot ; by thee
   God is made our ally ;
And man's inferior essence he
   With his did dignify.

For coalescent by that band
   We are his body grown,
Nourished with favours from his hand
   Whom from our head we own.

And such a knot, what arm dares loose,
   What life, what death can sever ?
Which us in him, and him in us,
   United keeps for ever.

LVI.

THEY are all gone into the world of light !
    And I alone sit lingering here ;
Their very memory is fair and bright,
    And my sad thoughts doth clear.

It glows and glitters in my cloudy breast,
    Like stars upon some gloomy grove,
Or those faint beams in which this hill is dressed,
    After the sun's remove.

I see them walking in an air of glory,
    Whose light doth trample on my days ;
My days, which are at best but dull and hoary,
    Mere glimmering and decays.

O holy Hope ! and high Humility !
    High as the heavens above !
These are your walks, and you have showed them me,
    To kindle my cold love.

Dear beauteous death ! the jewel of the just,
    Shining no where, but in the dark ;

What mysteries do lie beyond thy dust ;
  Could man out-look that mark !

He that hath found some fledged bird's nest, may know
  At first sight, if the bird be flown ;
But what fair well or grove he sings in now,
  That is to him unknown.

And yet as angels in some brighter dreams
  Call to the soul, when man doth sleep ;
So some strange thoughts transcend our wonted themes,
  And into glory peep.

If a star were confined into a tomb
  Her captive flames must needs burn there ;
But when the hand that locked her up, gives room,
  She'll shine through all the sphere.

O ! Father of eternal life, and all
  Created glories under thee,
Resume thy spirit from this world of thrall
  Into true liberty.

Either disperse these mists, which blot and fill
  My perspective, still, as they pass ;
Or else remove me hence unto that hill,
  Where I shall need no glass.

LVII.

PEACE.

M Y soul, there is a country
      Far beyond the stars,
Where stands a winged sentry
    All skilful in the wars ;
There, above noise and danger,
    Sweet Peace sits crowned with smiles,
And One born in a manger
    Commands the beauteous files.
He is thy gracious friend
    And, O my soul awake !
Did in pure love descend
    To die here for thy sake ;
If thou canst get but thither,
    There grows the flower of peace,
The rose that cannot wither,
    Thy fortress and thy ease.
Leave then thy foolish ranges,
    For none can thee secure,
But One, who never changes,
    Thy God, thy life, thy cure.

LVIII.

PATRICK CAREY,
born circa 1622.

A TRIOLET.

WORLDLY designs, fears, hopes, farewell !
  Farewell all earthly joys and cares !
On nobler thoughts my soul shall dwell,
Worldly designs, fears, hopes, farewell !
At quiet, in my peaceful cell,
I'll think on God, free from your snares ;
Worldly designs, fears, hopes, farewell !
Farewell all earthly joys and cares.

I'll seek my God's law to fulfil,
Riches and power I'll set at nought ;
Let others strive for them that will,
I'll seek my God's law to fulfil :
Lest sinful pleasures my soul kill,
By folly's vain delights first caught,
I'll seek my God's law to fulfil,
Riches and power I'll set at nought.

Yes, my dear Lord ! I've found it so ;
No joys but thine are purely sweet ;

Other delights come mixed with woe,
Yes, my dear Lord ! I've found it so.
Pleasure at courts is but in show,
With true content in cells we meet ;
Yes, my dear Lord ! I've found it so,
No joys but thine are purely sweet.

LIX.

'The invisible things of him from the creation of the world are
clearly seen, being understood by the things that are made.'

Rom. i. 20.

WHILST I beheld the neck of the dove,
    I spied, and read these words.
This pretty dye,
Which takes your eye,
Is not at all the bird's.
The dusky raven might
Have with these colours pleased your sight,
Had God but chose so to ordain above :
This label wore the dove.

Whilst I admired the nightingale,
These notes she warbled o'er.

No melody
Indeed have I,
Admire me then no more :
God has it in his choice
To give the owl, or me this voice ;
'Tis he, 'tis he that makes me tell my tale :
This sang the nightingale.

I smelt and praised the fragrant rose ;
Blushing, thus answered she.
The praise you gave,
The scent I have,
Do not belong to me ;
This harmless odour, none
But only God indeed does own ;
To be his keepers, my poor leaves he chose :
And thus replied the rose.

I took the honey from the bee ;
On the bag these words were seen.
More sweet than this
Perchance nought is,
Yet gall it might have been :
If God it should so please,
He could still make it such with ease ;
And as well gall to honey change can he :
This learnt I of the bee.

I touched, and liked the down of the swan ;
But felt these words there writ.
Bristles, thorns, here
I soon should bear,
Did God ordain but it ;
If my down to thy touch
Seem soft and smooth, God made it such ;
Give more, or take all this away, he can ;
This was I taught by the swan.

All creatures then, confess to God
That they owe him all, but I.
My senses find
True, what my mind
Would still, oft does deny.
Hence pride ! out of my soul !
O'er it thou shalt no more control ;
I'll learn this lesson, and escape the rod :
I too, have all from God.

LX.

FALLAX ET INSTABILIS.

'There is nothing new under the sun.'   *Eccl.* i. 10.

'TIS a strange thing this world,
    Nothing but change I see :
And yet it is most true
That in 't there's nothing new,
Though all seem new to me.
The rich become oft poor,
And heretofore 'twas so ;
The poor man rich doth grow,
And so 'twas heretofore ;
Nor is it a new thing
To have a subject made a king ;
Or that a king should from his throne be hurled.
'Tis a strange thing this world.

All things below do change,
The sea in rest ne'er lies ;
Ne'er lay in rest, nor will :
The weather alters still,
And ne'er did otherwise.

Consumed is many a town
By fire ; how, none can tell :
Plains up to mountains swell,
While mountains do sink down.
Yet ought we not to admire
The sea, the air, the earth, or fire :
The sun does think nothing of all this strange ;
Since all things here still change.

Let none then fix his heart
Upon such trifling toys;
But seek some object out,
Whose change he ne'er may doubt ;
There, let him place his joys.
Since that our souls are made
For ever to endure ;
Of chiefest grief we are sure,
If what we love must fade :
For friends feel greatest pain
When one must go, the other remain.
With what I love then, that I ne'er may part,
On God I'll fix my heart.

JOHN DRYDEN,
1631—1700.

LXI.

PARAPHRASE OF 'VENI CREATOR SPIRITUS.'

CREATOR Spirit ! by whose aid
The world's foundations first were laid,
Come visit every pious mind ;
Come pour thy joys on human kind ;
From sin and sorrow set us free,
And make thy temples worthy thee.

O source of uncreated light,
The Father's promised Paraclete !
Thrice holy fount, thrice holy fire,
Our hearts with heavenly love inspire ;
Come, and thy sacred unction bring
To sanctify us, while we sing.

Plenteous of grace, descend from high,
Rich in thy sevenfold energy !
Thou strength of his almighty hand,
Whose power does heaven and earth command.
Proceeding Spirit, our defence,

Who dost the gift of tongues dispense,
And crown'st thy gift with eloquence !

Refine and purge our earthly parts ;
But, O, inflame and fire our hearts !
Our frailties help, our vice control,
Submit the senses to the soul ;
And when rebellious they are grown,
Then lay thy hand, and hold them down.

Chase from our minds the infernal foe,
And peace, the fruit of love, bestow ;
And, lest our feet should step astray,
Protect, and guide us in the way.

Make us eternal truths receive,
And practise all that we believe :
Give us thyself, that we may see
The Father and the Son by thee.

Immortal honour, endless fame,
Attend the almighty Father's name :
The Saviour Son be glorified,
Who for lost man's redemption died :
And equal adoration be,
Eternal Paraclete, to thee.

JOHN NORRIS,
1657—1711.

LXII.

THE PROSPECT.

WHAT a strange moment will that be,
  My soul, how full of curiosity
When winged, and ready for thy eternal flight
On the utmost edges of thy tottering clay,
Hovering and wishing longer stay,
  Thou shalt advance, and have eternity in sight !
When just about to try that unknown sea,
What a strange moment will that be !

But yet how much more strange that state
When, loosened from the embrace of this close mate,
  Thou shalt at once be plunged in liberty,
And move as free and active as a ray
Shot from the lucid spring of day !
  Thou who just now wast clogged with dull mortality,
How wilt thou bear the mighty change, how know
Whether thou'rt then the same or no !

Then to strange mansions of the air
And stranger company must thou repair !

I

What a new scene of things will then appear !
The world thou by degrees wast taught to know,
Which lessened thy surprise below ;
But knowledge all at once will overflow thee there.
That world, as the first man did this, thou'lt see,
Ripe grown, in full maturity.

There with bright splendours must thou dwell,
And be what—only those pure forms can tell.
There must thou live awhile, gaze and admire,
Till the great angel's trump this fabric shake,
And all the slumbering dead awake,
Then to thy old, forgotten state thou must retire.
This union then will seem as strange, or more,
Than thy new liberty before.

Now for the greatest change prepare,
To see the only great, the only fair,
Veil now thy feeble eyes, gaze and be blest ;
Here all thy turns and revolutions cease,
Here's all serenity and peace :
Thou'rt to the centre come, the native seat of rest.
There's now no further change nor need there be ;
When one shall be variety.

JOSEPH ADDISON,
1672—1719.

LXIII.

A PASTORAL ODE.

THE Lord my pasture shall prepare,
  And feed me with a shepherd's care ;
His presence shall my wants supply,
And guard me with a watchful eye ;
My noon-day walks he shall attend,
And all my midnight hours defend.

When in the sultry glebe I faint,
Or on the thirsty mountain pant ;
To fertile vales and dewy meads
My weary, wandering steps he leads ;
Where peaceful rivers, soft and slow,
Amid the verdant landscape flow.

Though in the paths of death I tread,
With gloomy horrors overspread,
My steadfast heart shall fear no ill,
For thou, O Lord, art with me still ;
Thy friendly crook shall give me aid,
And guide me through the dreadful shade.

Though in a bare and rugged way,
Through devious lonely wilds I stray,
Thy bounty shall my pains beguile ;
The barren wilderness shall smile
With sudden greens and herbage crowned,
And streams shall murmur all around.

Isaac Watts.
1674—1748.

LXIV.

THE CHARACTERS OF CHRIST.

G O, worship at Immanuel's feet,
See in his face what wonders meet !
Earth is too narrow to express
His worth, his glory, or his grace.

The whole creation can afford
But some faint shadows of my Lord ;
Nature, to make his beauties known,
Must mingle colours not her own.

Is he compared to wine or bread ?
Dear Lord, our souls would thus be fed :
That flesh, that dying blood of thine,
Is bread of life, is heavenly wine.

Is he a tree ? The world receives
Salvation from his healing leaves :
That righteous branch, that fruitful bough
Is David's root and offspring too.

Is he a rose? Not Sharon yields
Such fragrancy in all her fields :
Or if the lily he assume
The valleys bless the rich perfume.

Is he a vine? His heavenly root
Supplies the boughs with life and fruit :
O let a lasting union join
My soul to Christ, the living vine !

Is he the head? Each member lives
And owns the vital powers he gives ;
The saints below, and saints above,
Joined by his Spirit and his love.

Is he a fountain? There I bathe,
And heal the plague of sin and death ;
These waters all my soul renew,
And cleanse my spotted garments too.

Is he a fire? He'll purge my dross ;
But the true gold sustains no loss :
Like a refiner shall he sit,
And tread the refuse with his feet.

Is he the rock? How firm he proves !
The Rock of Ages never moves ;

Yet the sweet streams that from him flow
Attend us all the desert through.

Is he a way?   He leads to God,
The path is drawn in lines of blood ;
There would I walk with hope and zeal,
Till I arrive at Sion's hill.

Is he a door?   I'll enter in ;
Behold the pastures large and green ;
A paradise divinely fair,
None but the sheep have freedom there.

Is he designed a corner stone
For men to build their heaven upon?
I'll make him my foundation too,
Nor fear the plots of hell below.

Is he a temple?   I adore
The indwelling majesty and power ;
And still to this most holy place
Whene'er I pray, I turn my face.

Is he a star?   He breaks the night,
Piercing the shades with dawning light ;
I know his glories from afar,
I know the bright, the morning star.

Is he a sun ?   His beams are grace,
IIis course is joy, and righteousness :
Nations rejoice when he appears
To chase their clouds, and dry their tears.

O let me climb those higher skies,
Where storms and darkness never rise !
There he displays his powers abroad,
And shines and reigns the incarnate God.

Nor earth, nor seas, nor sun, nor stars,
Nor heaven his full resemblance bears ;
IIis beauties we can never trace,
Till we behold him face to face.

LXV.

THE CROSS.

WHEN I survey the wondrous cross
    On which the Prince of glory died,
My richest gain I count but loss,
    And pour contempt on all my pride.

Forbid it, Lord, that I should boast,
    Save in the death of Christ my God ;

All the vain things that charm me most,
    I sacrifice them to his blood.

See from his head, his hands, his feet,
    Sorrow and love flow mingled down !
Did e'er such love and sorrow meet ?
    Or thorns compose so rich a crown ?

His dying crimson, like a robe,
    Spreads o'er his body on the tree ;
Then am I dead to all the globe,
    And all the globe is dead to me.

Were the whole realm of nature mine,
    That were a present far too small ;
Love so amazing, so divine,
    Demands my soul, my life, my all.

LXVI.

LAUNCHING INTO ETERNITY.

IT was a brave attempt ! adventurous he,
Who in the first ship broke the unknown sea,
And leaving his dear native shores behind,
Trusted his life to the licentious wind.

I see the surging brine : the tempest raves :
He on a pine plank rides across the waves,
Exulting on the edge of thousand gaping graves :
He steers the winged boat, and shifts the sails,
Conquers the flood, and manages the gales.

Such is the soul that leaves this mortal land,
Fearless when the great Master gives command.
Death is the storm : she smiles to hear it roar,
And bids the tempest waft her from the shore :
Then with a skilful helm she sweeps the seas,
And manages the raging storm with ease ;
Her faith can govern death, she spreads her wings
Wide to the wind, and as she sails she sings,
And loses by degrees the sight of mortal things.
As the shores lessen, so her joys arise ;
The waves roll gentler, and the tempest dies :
How vast eternity fills all her sight !
She floats on the broad deep with infinite delight,
The seas for ever calm, the skies for ever bright.

LXVII.

PSALM XC.

OUR God, our help in ages past,
    Our hope for years to come ;
Our shelter from the stormy blast,
    And our eternal home.

Under the shadow of thy throne
    Thy saints have dwelt secure ;
Sufficient is thine arm alone,
    And our defence is sure.

Before the hills in order stood,
    Or earth received her frame,
From everlasting thou art God,
    To endless years the same.

Thy word commands our flesh to dust,
    ' Return, ye sons of men : '
All nations rose from earth at first,
    And turn to earth again.

A thousand ages in thy sight
  Are like an evening gone ;
Short as the watch that ends the night
  Before the rising sun.

The busy tribes of flesh and blood,
  With all their lives and cares,
Are carried downwards by thy flood,
  And lost in following years.

Time like an ever-rolling stream,
  Bears all its sons away ;
They fly, forgotten as a dream
  Dies at the opening day.

Like flowery fields the nations stand,
  Pleased with the morning light :
The flowers beneath the mower's hand
  Lie withering ere 'tis night.

Our God, our help in ages past,
  Our hope for years to come,
Be thou our guard while troubles last,
  And our eternal home.

LXVIII.

HEAVEN.

THERE is a land of pure delight,
　　Where saints immortal reign ;
Infinite day excludes the night,
　　And pleasures banish pain.

There everlasting spring abides,
　　And never-withering flowers :
Death, like a narrow sea, divides
　　This heavenly land from ours.

Sweet fields beyond the swelling flood
　　Stand dressed in living green ;
So to the Jews old Canaan stood,
　　While Jordan rolled between.

But timorous mortals start and shrink,
　　To cross this narrow sea,
And linger, shivering on the brink,
　　And fear to launch away.

O ! could we make our doubts remove
    Those gloomy doubts that rise,
And see the Canaan that we love
    With unbeclouded eyes :

Could we but climb where Moses stood,
    And view the landscape o'er,
Not Jordan's stream, nor death's cold flood,
    Should fright us from the shore.

THOMAS PARNELL,
LXIX.   1679—1718.

ON DIVINE LOVE.

H OLY Jesus ! God of Love !
　 Look with pity from above ;
Shed the precious purple tide
From thine hands, thy feet, thy side ;
Let thy streams of comfort roll,
Let them please and fill my soul.
Let me thus for ever be
Full of gladness, full of thee.
This, for which my wishes pine,
Is the cup of love divine ;
Sweet affections flow from hence,
Sweet, above the joys of sense ;
Blessed philtre ! how we find
Its sacred worships ! how the mind,
Of all the world forgetful grown,
Can despise an earthly throne ;
Raise its thoughts to realms above,
Think of God, and sing of love.

Love celestial, wondrous heat,
O ! beyond expression great,

What resistless charms were thine,
In thy good, thy best design !
When God was hated, sin obeyed,
And man undone without thy aid,
From the seats of endless peace
They brought the Son, the Lord of grace ;
They taught him to receive a birth,
To clothe in flesh, to live on earth ;
And after, lifted him on high,
And taught him on the cross to die.

Love celestial, ardent fire,
O ! extreme of sweet desire,
Spread thy brightly raging flame
Through and over all my frame ;
Let it warm me, let it burn,
Let my corpse to ashes turn ;
And might thy flame thus act with me
To set the soul from body free,
I next would use thy wings, and fly
To meet my Jesus in the sky.

ALEXANDER POPE,
1688—1744.

LXX.

THE DYING CHRISTIAN TO HIS SOUL.

VITAL spark of heavenly flame ;
Quit, O quit this mortal frame :
Trembling, hoping, lingering, flying,
O the pain, the bliss of dying.
Cease, fond Nature, cease thy strife,
And let me languish into life.

Hark ! they whisper ; angels say,
Sister spirit, come away.
What is this absorbs me quite ?
Steals my senses, shuts my sight,
Drowns my spirits, draws my breath ?
Tell me, my soul, can this be death ?

The world recedes ; it disappears !
Heaven opens on my eyes ! my ears
With sounds seraphic ring :
Lend, lend your wings ! I mount ! I fly !
O grave ! where is thy victory?
O death ! where is thy sting?

K

LXXI.

THE UNIVERSAL PRAYER. DEO OPT. MAX.

FATHER of all ! in every age,
  In every clime adored,
By saint, by savage, and by sage,
  Jehovah, Jove, or Lord !

Thou Great First Cause, least understood :
  Who all my sense confined
To know but this, that thou art good,
  And that myself am blind ;

Yet gave me, in this dark estate,
  To see the good from ill ;
And binding Nature fast in fate,
  Left free the human will.

What conscience dictates to be done,
  Or warns me not to do,
This, teach me more than hell to shun,
  That, more than heaven pursue.

What blessings thy free bounty gives,
  Let me not cast away ;

For God is paid when man receives,
    To enjoy is to obey.

Yet not to earth's contracted span
    Thy goodness let me bound,
Or think thee Lord alone of man,
    When thousand worlds are round :

Let not this weak, unknowing hand
    Presume thy bolts to throw,
And deal damnation round the land,
    On each I judge thy foe.

If I am right, thy grace impart,
    Still in the right to stay ;
If I am wrong, O ! teach my heart
    To find that better way.

Save me alike from foolish pride,
    Or impious discontent,
At aught thy wisdom has denied,
    Or aught thy goodness lent.

Teach me to feel another's woe,
    To hide the fault I see ;
That mercy I to others shew,
    That mercy shew to me.

Mean though I am, not wholly so,
　Since quickened by thy breath;
O lead me wheresoe'er I go,
　Through this day's life or death.

This day be bread and peace my lot:
　All else beneath the sun,
Thou knowest if best bestowed or not,
　And let thy will be done.

To thee, whose temple is all space,
　Whose altar, earth, sea, skies!
One chorus let all Being raise!
　All Nature's incense rise!

JOHN BYROM,
1691—1763.

LXXII.

A HYMN TO JESUS.

COME, Saviour Jesus ! from above,
   Assist me with thy heavenly grace ;
Withdraw my heart from worldly love,
   And for thyself prepare the place.

Lord ! let thy sacred presence fill,
   And set my longing spirit free ;
That pants to have no other will,
   But night and day to think on thee.

Where'er thou leadest, I'll pursue,
   Through all retirements or employs ;
But to the world I'll bid adieu,
   And all its vain delusive joys.

That way with humble speed I'll walk,
   Wherein my Saviour's footsteps shine ;
Nor will I hear, nor will I talk
   Of any other love but thine.

To thee my longing heart aspires ;
   To thee I offer all my vows :

Keep me from false and vain desires,
My God, my Saviour, and my Spouse !

Henceforth, let no profane delight
Divide this consecrated soul !
Possess it thou, who hast the right,
As Lord and Master of the whole.

Wealth, honours, pleasures, or what else
This short enduring world can give,
Tempt as they will, my heart repels,
To thee alone resolved to live.

Thee we may love, and thee alone,
With inward peace and holy bliss ;
And when thou tak'st us for thy own,
O ! what a happiness is this.

Nor heaven nor earth do I desire,
Nor mysteries to be revealed ;
'Tis love that sets my heart on fire :
Speak thou the word, and I am healed.

All other graces I resign ;
Pleased to receive, pleased to restore :
Grace is thy gift, it shall be mine
The giver only to adore.

JOHN WESLEY,
1703—1791.

LXXIII.

GOD'S LOVE AND POWER.

I FELT my heart, and found a chillness cool
   Its purple channels in my frozen side ;
The spring was now become a standing pool,
   Deprived of motion and its active tide.
        O, stay ! O, stay !
I ever freeze if banished from thy ray:
A lasting warmth thy secret beams beget ;
Thou art a Sun which cannot rise or set.

Then thaw this ice, and make my frost retreat,
   But let with temperate rays thy lustre shine :
Thy judgment's lightning, but thy love is heat ;
   Those would consume my heart, but this refine.
        Inspire ! inspire !
And melt my soul with thy more equal fire ;
So shall a pensive deluge drown my fears,
My ice turn water, and dissolve in tears.

After thy love, if I continue hard,
   If sin again knit and confirmed be grown,

If guilt rebel, and stand upon his guard,
And what was ice before freeze into stone ;
    Reprove ! reprove !
Thy power assist thee to revenge thy love.
Lo, thou hast still thy threats and thunder left ;
The heart that can't be melted may be cleft !

LXXIV.

J ESU, if still the same thou art,
        If all thy promises are sure,
Set up thy kingdom in my heart,
    And make me rich, for I am poor :
To me be all thy treasures given,
The kingdom of an inward heaven.

Thou hast pronounced the mourner blest,
    And, lo ! for thee I ever mourn :
I cannot,—no ! I will not rest,
    Till thou my only Rest return ;
Till thou, the Prince of Peace, appear,
And I receive the Comforter.

Where is the blessedness bestowed
    On all that hunger after thee ?

I hunger now, I thirst for God !
  See, the poor, fainting sinner see,
And satisfy with endless peace,
And fill me with thy righteousness.

Ah, Lord !—If thou art in that sigh,
  Then hear thyself within me pray.
Hear in my heart thy Spirit's cry,
  Mark what my labouring soul would say ;
Answer the deep, unuttered groan,
And show that thou and I are one.

Shine on thy work, disperse the gloom,
  Light in thy light I then shall see :
Say to my soul, ' Thy light is come,
  Glory divine is risen on thee,
Thy warfare 's past, thy mourning 's o'er :
Look up ; for thou shalt weep no more.'

Lord, I believe the promise sure,
  And trust thou wilt not long delay ;
Hungry, and sorrowful, and poor,
  Upon thy word myself I stay ;
Into thy hands my all resign,
And wait—till all thou art is mine !

CHARLES WESLEY,
LXXV.   1708—1788.

WRESTLING JACOB.

COME, O ! thou Traveller unknown,
   Whom still I hold, but cannot see ;
My company before is gone,
   And I am left alone with thee ;
With thee all night I mean to stay,
And wrestle till the break of day.

I need not tell thee who I am,
   My misery or sin declare :
Thyself hast called me by my name ;
   Look on thy hands, and read it there.
But who, I ask thee, who art thou ?
Tell me thy name, and tell me now.

In vain thou strugglest to get free ;
   I never will unloose my hold.
Art thou the Man that died for me ?
   The secret of thy love unfold :
Wrestling, I will not let thee go,
Till I thy name, thy nature know.

Wilt thou not yet to me reveal
   Thy new, unutterable name?
Tell me, I still beseech thee, tell ;
   To know it now resolved I am :
Wrestling, I will not let thee go,
Till I thy name, thy nature know.

'Tis all in vain to hold thy tongue,
   Or touch the hollow of my thigh :
Though every sinew be unstrung,
   Out of my arms thou shalt not fly;
Wrestling, I will not let thee go,
Till I thy name, thy nature know.

What though my shrinking flesh complain,
   And murmur to contend so long?
I rise superior to my pain :
   When I am weak, then I am strong :
And when my all of strength shall fail,
I shall with the God-man prevail.

My strength is gone, my nature dies ;
   I sink beneath thy weighty hand ;
Faint to revive, and fall to rise :
   I fall, and yet by faith I stand.
I stand, and will not let thee go,
Till I thy name, thy nature know.

Yield to me now, for I am weak,
But confident in self-despair;
Speak to my heart, in blessings speak;
Be conquered by my instant prayer:
Speak, or thou never hence shalt move,
And tell me if thy name is Love.

'Tis Love! 'tis Love! thou diedst for me;
I hear thy whisper in my heart.
The morning breaks, the shadows flee;
Pure, universal Love thou art:
To me, to all, thy bowels move;
Thy nature and thy name is Love.

My prayer hath power with God; the grace
Unspeakable I now receive;
Through faith I see thee face to face;
I see thee face to face, and live.
In vain I have not wept and strove;
Thy nature and thy name is Love.

I know thee, Saviour, who thou art,
Jesus, the feeble sinner's friend;
Nor wilt thou with the night depart,
But stay and love me to the end:
Thy mercies never shall remove;
Thy nature and thy name is Love.

The Sun of Righteousness on me
   Hath rose, with healing in his wings ;
Withered my nature's strength ; from thee
   My soul its life and succour brings.
My help is all laid up above :
Thy nature and thy name is Love.

Contented now, upon my thigh
   I halt, till life's short journey end ;
All helplessness, all weakness, I
   On thee alone for strength depend ;
Nor have I power from thee to move :
Thy nature and thy name is Love.

Lame as I am, I take the prey ;
   Hell, earth, and sin, with ease o'ercome ;
I leap for joy, pursue my way,
   And as a bounding hart fly home,
Through all eternity to prove
Thy nature and thy name is Love.

LXXVI.

THE TRUE USE OF MUSIC.

L ISTED into the cause of sin,
    Why should a good be evil ?
Music, alas ! too long has been
    Prest to obey the devil :
Drunken, or lewd, or light the lay
    Flowed to the soul's undoing,
Widened, and strewed with flowers the way
    Down to eternal ruin.

Who on the part of God will rise,
    Innocent sound recover,
Fly on the prey, and take the prize,
    Plunder the carnal lover,
Strip him of every moving strain,
    Of every melting measure,
Music in virtue's cause retain,
    Rescue the holy pleasure ?

Come let us try if Jesu's love
    Will not as well inspire us :
This is the theme of those above,
    This upon earth shall fire us.

Say, if your hearts are tuned to sing,
  Is there a subject greater?
Harmony all its strains may bring,
  Jesus's name is sweeter.

Jesus the soul of music is ;
  His is the noblest passion :
Jesus's name is joy and peace,
  Happiness and salvation :
Jesus's name the dead can raise,
  Shew us our sins forgiven,
Fill us with all the life of grace.
  Carry us up to heaven.

Who hath a right like us to sing,
  Us whom his mercy raises?
Merry our hearts, for Christ is king,
  Cheerful are all our faces :
Who of his love doth once partake
  He evermore rejoices :
Melody in our hearts we make,
  Melody with our voices.

He that a sprinkled conscience hath,
  He that in God is merry,
Let him sing psalms, the Spirit saith,
  Joyful, and never weary,

Offer the sacrifice of praise,
    Hearty, and never ceasing,
Spiritual songs and anthems raise,
    Honour, and thanks, and blessing.

Then let us in his praises join,
    Triumph in his salvation,
Glory ascribe to love divine,
    Worship and adoration.
Heaven already is begun,
    Opened in each believer ;
Only believe, and still sing on,
    Heaven is ours forever.

LXXVII.

A HYMN.

YE happy souls, no longer tost,
    Like us on life's tempestuous sea,
Who cannot now be shipwrecked, lost,
    Safe-landed in eternity,
Are mortals banished from your mind,
Or think ye of your friends behind ?

Released from all your wants and cares,
  What commerce can ye have with men ?
Ye need not now our useless prayers,
  Nor will we ask your succour vain ;
One only advocate we own,
And trust in Jesu's help alone.

Yet—for he bids us keep in view
  Your active faith, and patient hope—
As ye your Lord, we follow you,
  And wait for him to take us up,
Our closest friendship to improve,
Our fellowship with saints above.

Till then we hold your memory dear,
  Which now relieves our drooping heart :
Like us ye mourned and suffered here,
  Like us ye languished to depart,
And laboured on with painful strife,
And dragged the heavy load of life.

The world cast out your name like ours,
  And counted you not fit to live :
Exposed to all the infernal powers,
  Ye dared your master's lot receive,
Beneath his cross rejoiced to bow,
And drank the cup we drink of now.

L

Tempted, detained in sore distress,
  With all our fiery trials tried,
Lost in this howling wilderness,
  Troubled, perplexed on every side,
Ye prayed—in groans at Jesu's stay,
And still complained—ye could not pray.

Ye felt the cruel torturing fear
  Which now our soul asunder saws,
The doubt ye should not persevere,
  But scandalize the Saviour's cause,
Disgrace, and shame the friends of God,
And fall, and perish in your blood.

Men of like passions once ye were
  With us, who still ourselves bemoan ;
This inbred sin ye groaned to bear,
  And hoped relief from death alone,
As death alone could purge the stain,
And Christ had shed his blood in vain.

But, O ! your evil day is past,
  Accomplished is your warfare here,
And, more than conquerors at last,
  Our sad desponding hearts ye cheer,
Ye bid us still your steps pursue,
And we shall more than conquer too.

Encompassed with so great a cloud
  Of witnesses, who speak though dead,
We cast aside our every load,
  And follow where our Lord hath led,
With patience run the appointed race.
And die to see his glorious face.

LXXVIII.

A HYMN.

H APPY soul, that safe from harms
  Rests within his shepherd's arms !
Who his quiet shall molest,
Who shall violate his rest ?

Jesus doth his spirit bear,
Jesus takes his every care,
He who found the wandering sheep,
Jesus still delights to keep.

Dogs and wolves in vain appear,
Roaring lions still are near,
Ravening wolves unmoved he sees
Roaring in the wilderness.

Calm he eyes them from above,
Safe in his protector's love,
There he rests, and undismayed
Drops his arms, and hangs his head.

O that I might so believe,
Steadfastly to Jesus cleave,
On his only love rely,
Smile at the destroyer nigh !

Free from sin, and servile fear,
Have my Jesus ever near,
All his care rejoice to prove,
All his paradise of love.

Jesu, seek thy wandering sheep,
Bring me back, and lead, and keep,
Take on thee my every care,
Bear me, on thy bosom bear.

Let me know my shepherd's voice,
More and more in thee rejoice ;
More and more of thee receive,
Ever in thy spirit live :

Live, till all thy life I know,
Perfect in my Lord below,

Gladly then from earth remove,
Gathered to the fold above.

O that I at last may stand
With the sheep at thy right hand,
Take the crown so freely given,
Enter in by thee to heaven !

JOSEPH HART,
1712—1768.

LXXIX.

A DIALOGUE BETWEEN A BELIEVER
AND HIS SOUL.

BELIEVER.

COME, my soul, and let us try,
    For a little season,
Every burthen to lay by ;
    Come, and let us reason.
What is this that casts thee down?
    Who are those that grieve thee ?
Speak, and let the worst be known ;
    Speaking may relieve thee.

SOUL.

Oh ! I sink beneath the load
    Of my nature's evil ;
Full of enmity to God ;
    Captived by the devil :
Restless as the troubled seas ;
    Feeble, faint, and fearful ;
Plagued with every sore disease ;
    How can I be cheerful ?

BELIEVER.

Think on what thy Saviour bore
    In the gloomy garden,
Sweating blood at every pore,
    To procure thy pardon !
See him stretched upon the wood,
    Bleeding, grieving, crying ;
Suffering all the wrath of God ;
    Groaning, gasping, dying !

SOUL.

This by faith I sometimes view,
    And those views relieve me ;
But my sins return anew ;
    These are they that grieve me.
Oh ! I'm leprous, stinking, foul ;
    Quite throughout infected,
Have I not, if any soul,
    Cause to be dejected ?

BELIEVER.

Think how loud thy dying Lord
    Cried out 'It is finished !'
Treasure up that sacred word
    Whole and undiminished.
Doubt not ; he will carry on
    To its full perfection,

That good work he has begun.
Why then this dejection?

SOUL.

Faith, when void of works, is dead :
This the Scriptures witness :
And what works have I to plead,
Who am all unfitness?
All my powers are depraved,
Blind, perverse, and filthy :
If from death I'm fully saved,
Why am I not healthy?

BELIEVER.

Pore not on thyself too long,
Lest it sink thee lower.
Look to Jesus, kind as strong,
Mercy joined with power.
Every work that thou must do
Will thy gracious Saviour
For thee work, and in thee too,
Of his special favour.

SOUL.

Jesu's precious blood, once spilt,
I depend on solely

To release and clear my guilt ;
But I would be holy.

BELIEVER.

He that bought thee on the Cross
Can control thy nature,
Fully purge away thy dross,
Make thee a new creature.

SOUL.

That he can I nothing doubt,
Be it but his pleasure.

BELIEVER.

Though it be not done throughout,
May it not in measure ?

SOUL.

When that measure, far from great,
Still shall seem decreasing—

BELIEVER.

Faint not then ; but pray, and wait,
Never, never ceasing.

SOUL.

What, when prayer meets no regard ?

BELIEVER.

Still repeat it often.

SOUL.

But I feel myself so hard—

BELIEVER.

Jesus will thee soften.

SOUL.

But my enemies make head—

BELIEVER.

Let them closer drive thee.

SOUL.

But I'm cold, I'm dark, I'm dead—

BELIEVER.

Jesus will revive thee.

CHRISTOPHER SMART,
1722—1770.

LXXX.

HYMN TO THE SUPREME BEING.

WHEN Israel's ruler on the royal bed
    In anguish and in perturbation lay,
The down relieved not his anointed head,
    And rest gave place to horror and dismay.
Fast flowed the tears, high heaved each gasping sigh,
When God's own prophet thundered—Monarch, thou
    must die.

And must I go, the illustrious mourner cried,
    I who have served thee still in faith and truth,
Whose snow-white conscience no foul crime has dyed
    From youth to manhood, infancy to youth,
Like David, who have still revered thy word,
The sovereign of myself and servant of the Lord !

The judge almighty heard his suppliant's moan,
    Repealed his sentence, and his health restored ;
The beams of mercy on his temples shone,
    Shot from that heaven to which his sighs had soared ;
The sun retreated at his maker's nod,
And miracles confirm the genuine work of God.

But, O immortals ! what had I to plead
   When death stood o'er me with his threatening lance,
When reason left me in the time of need,
   And sense was lost in terror or in trance,
My sinking soul was with my blood inflamed,
And the celestial image sunk, defaced and maimed.

I sent back memory, in heedful guise,
   To search the records of preceding years ;
Home, like the raven to the ark, she flies,
   Croaking bad tidings to my trembling ears.
O sun ! again that thy retreat was made,
And threw my follies back into the friendly shade !

But who are they, that bid affliction cease !—
   Redemption and forgiveness, heavenly sounds !
Behold the dove that brings the branch of peace,
   Behold the balm that heals the gaping wounds—
Vengeance divine 's by penitence suppressed—
She struggles with the angel, conquers, and is blest.

Yet hold, presumption, nor too fondly climb,
   And thou too hold, O horrible despair !
In man humility 's alone sublime,
   Who diffidently hopes he's Christ's own care—
O all-sufficient Lamb ! in death's dread hour
Thy merits who shall slight, or who can doubt thy power ?

But soul-rejoicing health again returns,
   The blood meanders gentle in each vein,
The lamp of life renewed with vigour burns,
   And exiled reason takes her seat again—
Brisk leaps the heart, the mind 's at large once more,
To love, to praise, to bless, to wonder and adore.

The virtuous partner of my nuptial bands,
   Appeared a widow to my frantic sight ;
My little prattlers lifting up their hands,
   Beckon me back to them, to life, and light ;
I come, ye spotless sweets ! I come again,
Nor have your tears been shed, nor have ye knelt in vain.

All glory to the Eternal, to the Immense,
   All glory to the Omniscient and Good,
Whose power 's uncircumscribed, whose love 's intense ;
   But yet whose justice ne'er could be withstood
Except through him—through him, who stands alone,
Of worth, of weight allowed for all mankind to atone !

He raised the lame, the lepers he made whole,
   He fixed the palsied nerves of weak decay,
He drove out Satan from the tortured soul,
   And to the blind gave or restored the day,—
Nay more,—far more unequalled pangs sustained,
Till his lost fallen flock his taintless blood regained.

My feeble feet refused my body's weight,
  Nor would my eyes admit the glorious light,
My nerves convulsed shook fearful of their fate,
  My mind lay open to the powers of night.
He pitying did a second birth bestow,—
A birth of joy—not like the first of tears and woe.

Ye strengthened feet, forth to his altar move ;
  Quicken, ye new-strung nerves, the enraptured lyre ;
Ye heaven-directed eyes, o'erflow with love ;
  Glow, glow, my soul, with pure seraphic fire ;
Deeds, thoughts, and words, no more his mandates break,
But to his endless glory work, conceive, and speak.

O ! penitence, to virtue near allied,
  Thou can'st new joys e'en to the blest impart ;
The listening angels lay their harps aside
  To hear the music of thy contrite heart ;
And heaven itself wears a more radiant face,
When charity presents thee to the throne of grace.

Chief of metallic forms is regal gold ;
  Of elements, the limpid fount that flows ;
Give me 'mongst gems the brilliant to behold ;
  O'er Flora's flock imperial is the rose :
Above all birds the sovereign eagle soars ;
And monarch of the field the lordly lion roars.

What can with great leviathan compare,
  Who takes his pastime in the mighty main ?
What, like the sun, shines through the realms of air,
  And gilds and glorifies the ethereal plain—
Yet what are these to man, who bears the sway ;
For all was made for him—to serve and to obey.

Thus in high heaven charity is great,
  Faith, hope, devotion, hold a lower place ;
On her the cherubs and the seraphs wait,
  Her, every virtue courts, and every grace ;
See ! on the right, close by the Almighty's throne,
In him she shines confessed, who came to make her known.

Deep rooted in my heart then let her grow,
  That for the past the future may atone ;
That I may act what thou hast given to know,
  That I may live for thee and thee alone,
And justify those sweetest words from heaven,
' That he shall love thee most to whom thou'st most
    forgiven.'

THOMAS OLIVER,
1725—1799.

LXXXI.

A HYMN.

THE God of Abraham praise,
     Who reigns enthroned above ;
Ancient of everlasting days,
     And God of love :
Jehovah, Great I Am !
     By earth and heaven confest ;
I bow and bless the sacred name,
     For ever blest.

The God of Abraham praise,
     At whose supreme command
From earth I rise and seek the joys
     At his right hand :
I all on earth forsake,
     Its wisdom, fame, and power ;
And him my only Portion make,
     My Shield and Tower.

The God of Abraham praise,
     Whose all-sufficient grace

Shall guide me all my happy days,
    In all my ways.
He calls a worm his friend,
He calls himself my God,
And he shall save me to the end
    Through Jesu's blood.

He by himself hath sworn,
    I on his oath depend ;
I shall, on eagles' wings upborne,
    To heaven ascend :
I shall behold his face,
I shall his power adore,
And sing the wonders of his grace
    For evermore.

Though nature's strength decay,
    And earth and hell withstand,
To Canaan's bounds I urge my way,
    At his command :
The watery deep I pass,
With Jesus in my view,
And through the howling wilderness
    My way pursue.

The goodly land I see,
    With peace and plenty blessed ;

M

A land of sacred liberty
And endless rest :
There milk and honey flow,
And oil and wine abound ;
And trees of life for ever grow,
With mercy crowned.

There dwells the Lord our King,
The Lord our righteousness,
Triumphant o'er the world and sin,
The Prince of peace :
On Sion's sacred height
His kingdom still maintains,
And glorious, with his saints in light,
For ever reigns.

He keeps his own secure,
He guards them by his side,
Arrays in garments white and pure
His spotless bride :
With streams of sacred bliss,
With groves of living joys,
With all the fruits of paradise,
He still supplies.

Before the **Three in One**,
They all exulting stand,

And tell the wonders he hath done
  Through all their land.
The listening spheres attend,
  And swell the growing fame,
And sing, in songs which never end,
  The wondrous Name.

  The God who reigns on high
  The great archangels sing,
And 'Holy, holy, holy,' cry,
  'Almighty King!
Who was, and is the same,
  And evermore shall be;
Jehovah—Father—great I Am!
  We worship thee.'

  Before the Saviour's face
  The ransomed nations bow;
O'erwhelmed at his almighty grace,
  For ever new:
He shows his prints of love;
  They kindle to a flame,
And sound, through all the worlds above,
  The slaughtered Lamb.

  The whole triumphant host
  Give thanks to God on high:

Hail, Father, Son, and Holy Ghost,
They ever cry :
Hail, Abraham's God and mine ;
I join the heavenly lays ;
All might and majesty are thine,
And endless praise.

GEORGE HORNE,
1730—1792.

LXXXII.

WRITTEN AT AN INN.

FROM much loved friends whene'er I part,
A pensive sadness fills my heart ;
Past scenes my fancy wanders o'er,
And sighs to think they are no more.

Along the road I musing go,
O'er many a deep and miry slough ;
The shrouded moon withdraws her light,
And leaves me to the gloomy night.

An inn receives me, where unknown
I solitary sit me down :
Many I hear, and some I see,
I nought to them, they nought to me.

Thus in these regions of the dead
A pilgrim's wandering life I lead,
And still at every step declare,
I've no abiding city here :

For very far from hence I dwell,
And therefore bid the world farewell,

Finding of all the joys it gives
A sad remembrance only lives.

Rough stumbling-stones my steps o'erthrow,
And lay a wandering sinner low ;
Yet still my course to heaven I steer,
Though neither moon nor stars appear !

The world is like an inn ; for there
Men call, and storm, and drink, and swear ;
While undisturbed a Christian waits,
And reads, and writes, and meditates.

Though in the dark oft times I stray,
The Lord shall light me on my way,
And to the city of the sun
Conduct me, when my journey 's done.

There by these eyes shall he be seen,
Who sojourned for me at an inn ;
On Sion's hill I those shall hail,
From whom I parted in the vale.

Why am I heavy then and sad
When thoughts like these should make me glad?
Muse then no more on things below ;
Arise my soul, and let us go.

LXXXIII.

William Cowper,
1731—1800.

SUBJOINED TO THE YEARLY BILL OF MORTALITY OF THE PARISH OF ALL SAINTS, NORTHAMPTON, 1792.

THANKLESS for favours from on high,
  Man thinks he fades too soon ;
Though 'tis his privilege to die,
  Would he improve the boon.

But he, not wise enough to scan
  His blessed concerns aright,
Would gladly stretch life's little span
  To ages, if he might.

To ages in a world of pain,
  To ages, where he goes
Galled by affliction's heavy chain,
  And hopeless of repose.

Strange fondness of the human heart,
  Enamoured of its harm !
Strange world, that costs it so much smart,
  And still has power to charm.

Whence has the world her magic power ?
Why deem we death a foe ?
Recoil from weary life's best hour,
And covet longer woe ?

The cause is conscience—conscience oft
Her tale of guilt renews :
Her voice is terrible though soft,
And dread of death ensues.

Then anxious to be longer spared,
Man mourns his fleeting breath :
All evils then seem light, compared
With the approach of death.

'Tis judgment shakes him ; there's the fear
That prompts the wish to stay :
He has incurred a long arrear,
And must despair to pay.

Pay!—follow Christ, and all is paid ;
His death your peace ensures ;
Think on the grave where he was laid,
And calm descend to yours.

LXXXIV.

AN ASPIRATION.

O ! for a closer walk with God,
    A calm and heavenly frame !
A light to shine upon the road
    That leads me to the Lamb !

Where is the blessedness I knew
    When first I saw the Lord ?
Where is the soul-refreshing view
    Of Jesus and his word ?

What peaceful hours I once enjoyed !
    How sweet their memory still !
But they have left an aching void
    The world can never fill.

Return, O holy Dove ! return,
    Sweet messenger of rest !
I hate the sins that made thee mourn,
    And drove thee from my breast.

The dearest idol I have known,
    Whate'er that idol be,

Help me to tear it from thy throne,
And worship only thee.

So shall my walk be close with God,
Calm and serene my frame ;
So purer light shall mark the road
That leads me to the Lamb !

LXXXV.

A HYMN.

GOD moves in a mysterious way
His wonders to perform ;
He plants his footsteps in the sea,
And rides upon the storm.

Deep in unfathomable mines
Of never-failing skill,
He treasures up his bright designs,
And works his sovereign will.

Ye fearful saints, fresh courage take ;
The clouds ye so much dread
Are big with mercy, and shall break
In blessings on your head.

Judge not the Lord by feeble sense,
   But trust him for his grace :
Behind a frowning providence
   He hides a smiling face.

His purposes will ripen fast,
   Unfolding every hour ;
The bud may have a bitter taste,
   But sweet will be the flower.

Blind unbelief is sure to err,
   And scan his work in vain ;
God is his own interpreter,
   And he will make it plain.

LXXXVI.

LOOKING UPWARDS IN A STORM.

GOD of my life, to thee I call ;
   Afflicted, at thy feet I fall ;
When the great water-floods prevail,
Leave not my trembling heart to fail !

Friend of the friendless and the faint,
Where should I lodge my deep complaint ?

Where but with thee, whose open door
Invites the helpless and the poor.

Did ever mourner plead with thee,
And thou refuse that mourner's plea?
Does not the word still fixed remain,
That none shall seek thy face in vain?

That were a grief I could not bear,
Didst thou not hear and answer prayer;
But a prayer-hearing, answering God,
Supports me under every load.

Fair is the lot that's cast for me;
I have an advocate with thee;
They whom the world caresses most
Have no such privilege to boast.

Poor though I am, despised, forgot,
Yet God, my God, forgets me not:
And he is safe, and must succeed,
For whom the Lord vouchsafes to plead.

LXXXVII.

'LOVEST THOU ME?'

H ARK, my soul! it is the Lord.
 'Tis thy Saviour; hear his word;
Jesus speaks, and speaks to thee;
' Say, poor sinner, lovest thou me?

' I delivered thee when bound,
And when bleeding, healed thy wound;
Sought thee wandering, set thee right;
Turned thy darkness into light.

' Can a woman's tender care
Cease towards the child she bare?
Yes, she may forgetful be,
Yet will I remember thee.

' Mine is an unchanging love,
Higher than the heights above,
Deeper than the depths beneath,
Free and faithful, strong as death.

' Thou shalt see my glory soon,
When the work of grace is done ;
Partner of my throne shalt be ;
Say, poor sinner, lovest thou me ?'

Lord, it is my chief complaint,
That my love is weak and faint ;
Yet I love thee and adore ;
O for grace to love thee more !

AUGUSTUS MONTAGUE TOPLADY,
1740—1778.

LXXXVIII.

A MORNING HYMN.

CHRIST whose glory fills the skies,
   Christ the true, the only light,
Son of righteousness arise,
   Triumph o'er the shades of night;
Day-spring from on high be near,
Day-star in my heart appear.

Dark and cheerless is the morn,
   Unaccompanied by thee :
Joyless is the day's return,
   Till thy mercy's beams I see :
Till they inward light impart,
Glad my eyes and warm my heart.

Visit then this soul of mine,
   Pierce the gloom of sin and grief,
Fill me, radiancy divine ;
   Scatter all my unbelief ;
More and more thyself display,
Shining to the perfect day.

LXXXIX.

A PRAYER, LIVING AND DYING.

ROCK of ages, cleft for me,
Let me hide myself in thee ;
Let the water and the blood,
From thy riven side which flowed,
Be of sin the double cure,
Cleanse me from its guilt and power.

Not the labours of my hands,
Can fulfil thy laws' demands :
Could my zeal no respite know,
Could my tears for ever flow ;
All for sin could not atone,
Thou must save, and thou alone.

Nothing in my hand I bring,
Simply to thy cross I cling ;
Naked come to thee for dress,
Helpless look to thee for grace :
Foul, I to the fountain fly,
Wash me, Saviour, or I die.

While I draw this fleeting breath,
While my eyestrings break in death ;
When I soar to worlds unknown,
See thee on thy judgment throne ;
Rock of ages, cleft for me,
Let me hide myself in thee.

ANNA LÆTITIA BARBAULD,
1743-1825.

XC.

PRAISE TO GOD.

PRAISE to God, immortal praise,
  For the love that crowns our days ;
Bounteous source of every joy,
Let thy praise our tongues employ.

For the blessings of the field,
For the stores the gardens yield,
For the vine's exalted juice,
For the generous olive's use.

Flocks that whiten all the plain,
Yellow sheaves of ripened grain ;
Clouds that drop their fattening dews
Suns that temperate warmth diffuse.

All that spring, with bounteous hand,
Scatters o'er the smiling land ;
All that liberal autumn pours
From her rich o'erflowing stores.

These to thee, my God, we owe,
Source whence all our blessings flow ;
And for these my soul shall raise
Grateful vows and solemn praise.

Yet should rising whirlwinds tear
From its stem the ripening ear ;
Should the fig-tree's blasted shoot
Drop her green untimely fruit ;

Should the vine put forth no more,
Nor the olive yield her store ;
Though the sickening flocks should fall,
And the herds desert the stall ;

Should thine altered hand restrain
The early and the latter rain,
Blast each opening bud of joy,
And the rising year destroy,—

Yet to thee my soul shall raise
Grateful vows and solemn praise ;
And when every blessing 's flown,
Love thee for thyself alone.

STANZAS IN THE PROSPECT OF DEATH.

WHY am I loth to leave this earthly scene?
   Have I so found it full of pleasing charms?
Some drops of joy with draughts of ill between :
   Some gleams of sunshine 'mid renewing storms :
Is it departing pangs my soul alarms?
   Or death's unlovely, dreary, dark abode?
For guilt, for guilt, my terrors are in arms ;
   I tremble to approach an angry God,
And justly smart beneath his sin-avenging rod.

Fain would I say, 'Forgive my foul offence ! '
   Fain promise never more to disobey ;
But, should my Author health again dispense,
   Again I might desert fair virtue's way ;
Again in folly's path might go astray ;
   Again exalt the brute and sink the man ;
Then how should I for heavenly mercy pray,
   Who act so counter heavenly mercy's plan?
Who sin so oft have mourned, yet to temptation ran.

O thou, great Governor of all below !
  If I may dare a lifted eye to thee,
Thy nod can make the tempest cease to blow,
  Or still the tumult of the raging sea :
With that controlling power assist even me,
  Those headlong furious passions to confine ;
For all unfit I feel my powers to be,
  To rule their torrent in the allowed line ;
  O ! aid me with thy help, Omnipotence Divine.

XCII.

JOSEPH GRIGG,
born 1768.

'BEHOLD! I STAND.'

BEHOLD! a Stranger's at the door!
He gently knocks, has knocked before;
Has waited long, is waiting still;
You treat no other friend so ill.

But will he prove a friend indeed?
He will; the very friend you need.
The Man of Nazareth, 'tis he!
With garments dyed at Calvary.

Oh lovely attitude! He stands
With melting heart and laden hands:
Oh matchless kindness! and he shows
This matchless kindness to his foes.

Rise! touched with gratitude divine,
Turn out his enemy and thine,—
That hateful, hell-born monster sin,
And let the heavenly Stranger in.

If thou art poor, and poor thou art,
Lo ! he has riches to impart ;
Not wealth, in which mean avarice rolls :
O better far, the wealth of souls !

Thou'rt blind, he'll take the scales away,
And let in everlasting day :
Naked thou art, but he shall dress
Thy blushing soul in righteousness.

Art thou a weeper ? Grief shall fly,
For who can weep with Jesus by ?
No terror shall thy hopes annoy,
No tear—except the tear of joy.

Admit him ; for the human breast
Ne'er entertained so kind a guest.
Admit him ; for you can't expel ;
Where'er he comes, he comes to dwell.

Admit him ; ere his anger burn,
His feet depart, ne'er to return ;
Admit him ; or the hour 's at hand,
When at his door denied you'll stand.

Yet know, nor of the terms complain,
If Jesus comes, he comes to reign ;

To reign, and with no partial sway ;
Thoughts must be slain that disobey.

Sovereign of souls ! Thou Prince of peace !
Oh may thy gentle reign increase !
Throw wide the door, each willing mind,
And be his empire all mankind.

XCIII.

WILLIAM WORDSWORTH,
1770—1850.

THE LABOURER'S NOON-DAY HYMN.

U P to the throne of God is borne
     The voice of praise at early morn,
And he accepts the punctual hymn
Sung as the light of day grows dim.

Nor will he turn his ear aside
From holy offerings at noon-tide.
Then here reposing let us raise
A song of gratitude and praise.

What though our burthen be not light,
We need not toil from morn to night ;
The respite of the mid-day hour
Is in the thankful creature's power.

Blest are the moments, doubly blest,
That, drawn from this one hour of rest,
Are with a ready heart bestowed
Upon the service of our God !

Why should we crave a hallowed spot ?
An altar is in each man's cot,

A church in every grove that spreads
Its living roof above our heads.

Look up to heaven ! the industrious sun
Already half his race hath run ;
He cannot halt nor go astray,
But our immortal spirits may.

Lord ! since his rising in the east,
If we have faltered or transgressed,
Guide, from thy love's abundant source,
What yet remains of this day's course :

Help with thy grace, through life's short day,
Our upward and our downward way ;
And glorify for us the west,
When we shall sink to final rest.

Sir Walter Scott,
1771—1832.

XCIV.

IN EXITU ISRAEL.

WHEN Israel, of the Lord beloved,
 Out from the land of bondage came,
Her fathers' God before her moved,
 An awful guide in smoke and flame.
By day, along the astonished lands
 The cloudy pillar glided slow ;
By night, Arabia's crimsoned sands
 Returned the fiery column's glow.

There rose the choral hymn of praise,
 And trump and timbrel answered keen,
And Zion's daughters poured their lays,
 With priest's and warrior's voice between.
No portents now our foes amaze,
 Forsaken Israel wanders lone :
Our fathers would not know thy ways,
 And thou hast left them to their own.

But present still, though now unseen !
 When brightly shines the prosperous day,

Be thoughts of thee a cloudy screen
   To temper the deceitful ray.
And O ! when stoops on Judah's path
   In shade and storm the frequent night,
Be thou, long-suffering, slow to wrath,
   A burning and a shining light.

Our harps we left by Babel's streams,
   The tyrant's jest, the Gentile's scorn ;
No censer round our altar beams,
   And mute are timbrel, harp, and horn.
But thou hast said, The blood of goat,
   The flesh of rams I will not prize ;
A contrite heart, a humble thought,
   Are mine accepted sacrifice.

XCV.

THOMAS CAMPBELL,
1777—1844.

THE NATIVITY.

WHEN Jordan hushed his waters still,
And silence slept on Zion hill ;
When Salem's shepherds through the night
Watched o'er their flocks by starry light :

Hark ! from the midnight hills around,
A voice, of more than mortal sound,
In distant hallelujahs stole,
Wild murmuring o'er the raptured soul.

Then swift to every startled eye,
New streams of glory gild the sky ;
Heaven bursts her azure gates, to pour
Her spirits to the midnight hour.

On wheels of light, on wings of flame,
The glorious hosts to Zion came ;
High heaven with songs of triumph rung,
While thus they smote their harps and sung :

O Zion ! lift thy raptured eye,
The long-expected hour is nigh ;

The joys of nature rise again,
The Prince of Salem comes to reign !

See Mercy, from her golden urn,
Pours a rich stream to them that mourn ;
Behold, she binds with tender care,
The bleeding bosom of despair.

He comes to cheer the trembling heart,
Bids Satan and his host depart ;
Again the day-star gilds the gloom,
Again the bowers of Eden bloom !

O Zion ! lift thy raptured eye,
The long-expected hour is nigh ;
The joys of nature rise again,
The Prince of Salem comes to reign !

XCVI.

THOMAS MOORE,
1779—1852

A SONG.

THE turf shall be my fragrant shrine ;
My temple, Lord ! that arch of thine ;
My censer's breath the mountain airs,
And silent thoughts my only prayers.

My choir shall be the moonlight waves,
When murmuring homeward to their caves,
Or when the stillness of the sea,
E'en more than music, breathes of thee !

I'll seek by day, some glade unknown,
All light and silence, like thy throne !
And the pale stars shall be, at night,
The only eyes that watch my rite.

Thy heaven, on which 'tis bliss to look,
Shall be my pure and shining book,
Where I shall read, in words of flame,
The glories of thy wondrous name.

I'll read thy anger in the rack
That clouds awhile the day-beam's track ;
Thy mercy in the azure hue
Of sunny brightness, breaking through.

There's nothing bright, above, below,
From flowers that bloom to stars that glow,
But in its light my soul can see
Some feature of thy deity :

There's nothing dark, below, above,
But in its gloom I trace thy love,
And meekly wait that moment, when
Thy touch shall turn all bright again !

XCVII.

THOU art, O God ! the life and light
    Of all this wondrous world we see ;
Its glow by day, its smile by night,
    Are but reflections caught from thee :
Where'er we turn thy glories shine,
And all things fair and bright are thine.

When day, with farewell beam, delays
   Among the opening clouds of even,
And we can almost think we gaze
   Through golden vistas into heaven ;
Those hues, that make the sun's decline
So soft, so radiant, Lord ! are thine.

When night, with wings of starry gloom,
   O'ershadows all the earth and skies,
Like some dark, beauteous bird, whose plume
   Is sparkling with unnumbered eyes ;
That sacred gloom, those fires divine,
So grand, so countless, Lord ! are thine.

When youthful spring around us breathes,
   Thy spirit warms her fragrant sigh ;
And every flower the summer wreathes
   Is born beneath that kindling eye.
Where'er we turn, thy glories shine,
And all things fair and bright are thine.

GEORGE CROLY,
1780—1860.
XCVIII.

A SUPPLICATION.

SPIRIT of God ! descend upon my heart ;
     Wean it from earth, though all its pulses move ;
Stoop to my weakness, mighty as thou art,
     And make me love thee, as I ought to love.

I ask no dream, no prophet ecstasies,
     No sudden rending of the veil of clay ;
No angel visitant, no opening skies ;—
     But take the dimness of the soul away.

Hast thou not bid us love thee, God and King ?
     All, all thine own—soul, heart, and strength, and mind ;
I see thy cross—there teach my heart to cling :
     O ! let me seek thee,—and O ! let me find !

Teach me to feel, that thou art always nigh ;
     Teach me the struggles of the soul to bear,
To check the rising doubt, the rebel sigh ;
     Teach me the patience of unanswered prayer.

I know thee glorious ! might and mercy all,
  All that commands thy creatures' boundless praise ;
Yet shall my soul from that high vision fall,
  Too cold to worship, and too weak to gaze ?

Teach me to love thee, as thine angels love,
  One holy passion filling all my frame ;
The baptism of the heaven-descended dove,
  My heart an altar, and thy love its flame.

XCIX.

REGINALD HEBER,
1783—1826.

A HYMN.

THE Lord of Might from Sinai's brow,
Gave forth his voice of thunder ;
And Israel lay on earth below,
Outstretched in fear and wonder.
Beneath his feet was pitchy night,
And at his left hand and his right,
The rocks were rent asunder.

The Lord of Love on Calvary,
A meek and suffering stranger,
Upraised to heaven his languid eye
In nature's hour of danger ;
For us he bore the weight of woe,
For us he gave his blood to flow,
And met his Father's anger.

The Lord of Love, the Lord of Might,
The King of all created,
Shall back return to claim his right,
On clouds of glory seated ;
With trumpet-sound, and angel-song,
And hallelujahs loud and long,
O'er death and hell defeated !

A HYMN.

CREATOR of the rolling flood !
   On whom thy people hope alone ;
Who cam'st by water and by blood,
   For man's offences to atone :

Who from the labours of the deep
   Didst set thy servant Peter free,
To feed on earth thy chosen sheep,
   And build an endless church for thee ;

Grant us, devoid of worldly care,
   And leaning on thy bounteous hand,
To seek thy help in humble prayer,
   And on thy sacred rock to stand :

And when, our livelong toil to crown,
   Thy call shall set the spirit free,
To cast with joy our burthen down,
   And rise, O Lord ! and follow thee !

CI.

A HYMN.

FORTH from the dark and stormy sky,
Lord, to thine altar's shade we fly ;
Forth from the world, its hope and fear,
Saviour, we seek thy shelter here :
Weary and weak, thy grace we pray :
Turn not, O Lord ! thy guests away !

Long have we roamed in want and pain,
Long have we sought thy rest in vain ;
Wildered in doubt, in darkness lost,
Long have our souls been tempest-tossed :
Low at thy feet our sins we lay ;
Turn not, O Lord ! thy guests away !

CII.

HENRY HART MILMAN,
1791—1868.

HYMN, FROM 'THE MARTYR OF ANTIOCH.'

FOR thou didst die for me, O Son of God !
  By thee the throbbing flesh of man was worn ;
Thy naked feet the thorns of sorrow trod,
  And tempests beat thy houseless head forlorn.
Thou, that wert wont to stand
Alone, on God's right hand,
  Before the ages were, the Eternal, eldest born.

Thy birthright in the word was pain and grief,
  Thy love's return in gratitude and hate ;
The limbs thou healedst brought thee no relief,
  The eyes thou openedst calmly viewed thy fate :
Thou, that wert wont to dwell
In peace, tongue cannot tell
  Nor heart conceive the bliss of thy celestial state.

They dragged thee to the Roman's solemn hall,
  Where the proud judge in purple splendour sate ;
Thou stoodst a meek and patient criminal,
  Thy doom of death from human lips to wait ;
Whose throne shall be the world
In final ruin hurled,
  With all mankind to hear their everlasting fate.

Thou wert alone in that fierce multitude
   When ' Crucify him ! ' yelled the general shout ;
No hand to guard thee 'mid those insults rude,
   Nor lip to bless in all that frantic rout ;
Whose lightest whispered word
The Seraphim had heard,
   And adamantine arms from all the heaven broke out.

They bound thy temples with the twisted thorn,
   Thy bruised feet went languid on with pain ;
Thy blood, from all thy flesh with scourges torn,
   Deepened thy robe of mockery's crimson grain ;
Whose native vesture bright
Was the unapproached light,
   The sandal of whose foot the rapid hurricane.

They smote thy cheek with many a ruthless palm,
   With the cold spear thy shuddering side they pierced ;
The draught of bitterest gall was all the balm
   They gave, to enhance thy unslaked, burning thirst :
Thou at whose words of peace
Did pain and anguish cease,
   And the long-buried dead their bonds of slumber burst.

Low bowed thy head convulsed and drooped in death,
   Thy voice sent forth a sad and wailing cry ;
Slow struggled from thy breast the parting breath,
   And every limb was wrung with agony :

That head, whose veilless blaze
Filled angels with amaze,
    When at that voice sprang forth the rolling suns on
    high.

And thou wert laid within the narrow tomb,
    Thy clay-cold limbs with shrouding grave-clothes
    bound ;
The sealed stone confirmed thy mortal doom,
    Lone watchmen walked thy desert burial-ground,
Whom heaven could not contain,
Nor the immeasurable plain
    Of vast infinity inclose or circle round.

For us, for us, thou didst endure the pain,
    And thy meek spirit bowed itself to shame,
To wash our souls from sin's infecting stain,
    To avert the Father's wrathful vengeance flame :
Thou that could'st nothing win
By saving worlds from sin,
    Nor aught of glory add to thy all-glorious name.

CIII.

HYMN.

WHEN our heads are bowed with woe,
When our bitter tears o'erflow ;
When we mourn the lost, the dear,
Gracious Son of Mary, hear !

Thou our throbbing flesh hast worn,
Thou our mortal griefs hast borne,
Thou hast shed the human tear :
Gracious Son of Mary, hear !

When the sullen death-bell tolls
For our own departed souls,
When our final doom is near,
Gracious Son of Mary, hear !

Thou hast bowed the dying head ;
Thou the blood of life hast shed ;
Thou hast filled a mortal bier :
Gracious Son of Mary, hear !

When the heart is sad within
With the thought of all its sin ;
When the spirit shrinks with fear,
Gracious Son of Mary, hear !

Thou the shame, the grief, hast known,
Though the sins were not thine own ;
Thou hast deigned their load to bear ;
Gracious Son of Mary, hear !

JOHN KEBLE,
CIV.   1792—1866.

CHRIST IN THE GARDEN.

O LORD my God, do thou thy holy will—
  I will lie still—
I will not stir, lest I forsake thine arm,
 And break the charm,
Which lulls me, clinging to my Father's breast,
 In perfect rest.

Wild Fancy, peace ! thou must not me beguile
 With thy false smile :
I know thy flatteries and thy cheating ways ;
 Be silent, Praise,
Blind guide with siren voice, and blinding all
 That hear thy call.

Come, Self-devotion, high and pure,
Thoughts that in thankfulness endure,
Though dearest hopes are faithless found,
And dearest hearts are bursting round.
Come, Resignation, spirit meek,
And let me kiss thy placid cheek,
And read in thy pale eye serene

Their blessing, who by faith can wean
Their hearts from sense, and learn to love
God only, and the joys above.

They say, who know the life divine,
And upward gaze with eagle eyne,
That by each golden crown on high,
Rich with celestial jewelry,
Which for our Lord's redeemed is set,
There hangs a radiant coronet,
All gemmed with pure and living light,
Too dazzling for a sinner's sight,
Prepared for virgin souls, and them
Who seek the martyr's diadem.

Nor deem, who to that bliss aspire,
Must win their way through blood and fire.
The writhings of a wounded heart
Are fiercer than a foeman's dart.
Oft in life's stillest shade reclining,
In Desolation unrepining,
Without a hope on earth to find
A mirror in an answering mind,
Meek souls there are, who little dream
Their daily strife an angel's theme,
Or that the rod they take so calm
Shall prove in heaven a martyr's palm.

And there are souls that seem to dwell
Above this earth—so rich a spell
Floats round their steps, where'er they move,
From hopes fulfilled and mutual love.
Such, if on high their thoughts are set,
Nor in the stream the source forget,
If prompt to quit the bliss they know,
Following the Lamb where'er he go,
By purest pleasures unbeguiled
To idolize or wife or child ;
Such wedded souls our God shall own
For faultless virgins round his throne.

Thus everywhere we find our suffering God,
    And where he trod
May set our steps : the Cross on Calvary
    Uplifted high
Beams on the martyr host, a beacon light
    In open fight.

To the still wrestlings of the lonely heart
    He doth impart
The virtue of his midnight agony,
    When none was nigh,
Save God and one good angel, to assuage
    The tempest's rage.

Mortal ! if life smile on thee, and thou find
 All to thy mind,
Think, who did once from heaven to hell descend
 Thee to befriend :
So shalt thou dare forego, at his dear call,
 Thy best, thine all.

' O Father ! not my will, but thine be done '—
 So spake the Son.
Be this our charm, mellowing earth's ruder noise
 Of griefs and joys ;
That we may cling for ever to thy breast
 In perfect rest !

CV.

ISRAEL AMONG THE RUINS OF CANAAN.

WHERE is the land with milk and honey flowing,
 The promise of our God, our fancy's theme ?
Here over shattered walls dank weeds are growing,
 And blood and fire have run in mingled stream ;
  Like oaks and cedars all around
  The giant corses strew the ground,
And haughty Jericho's cloud-piercing wall
Lies where it sank at Joshua's trumpet call.

These are not scenes for pastoral dance at even,
  For moonlight rovings in the fragrant glades,
Soft slumbers in the open eye of heaven,
  And all the listless joy of summer shades.
    We in the midst of ruins live,
    Which every hour dread warning give,
Nor may our household vine or fig tree hide
The broken arches of old Canaan's pride.

Where is the sweet repose of hearts repenting,
  The deep calm sky, the sunshine of the soul,
Now heaven and earth are to our bliss consenting,
  And all the Godhead joins to make us whole?
    The triple crown of mercy now
    Is ready for the suppliant's brow,
By the Almighty Three for ever planned,
And from behind the cloud held out by Jesus' hand.

' Now Christians, hold your own—the land before ye
  Is open—win your way, and take your rest.'
So sounds our war-note ; but our path of glory
  By many a cloud is darkened and unblest :
    And daily as we downward glide,
    Life's ebbing stream on either side
Shews at each turn some mouldering hope or joy,
The man seems following still the funeral of the boy.

Open our eyes, thou Sun of life and gladness,
 That we may see that glorious world of thine !
It shines for us in vain, while drooping sadness
 Enfolds us here like mist : come Power benign
  Touch our chilled hearts with vernal smile,
  Our wintry course do thou beguile,
Not by the wayside ruins let us mourn,
Who have the eternal towers for our appointed bourne.

CVI.

MOUNTAIN SCENERY.

WHERE is thy favoured haunt, eternal Voice,
  The region of thy choice,
Where, undisturbed by sin and earth, the soul
  Owns thine entire control ?—
'Tis on the mountain's summit dark and high,
  When storms are hurrying by :
'Tis 'mid the strong foundations of the earth,
  Where torrents have their birth.

No sounds of worldly toil ascending there,
  Mar the full burst of prayer ;
Lone Nature feels that she may freely breathe,
  And round us and beneath

P

Are heard her sacred tones : the fitful sweep
    Of winds across the steep,
Through withered bents—romantic note and clear,
    Meet for a hermit's ear,—

The wheeling kite's wild solitary cry,
    And, scarcely heard so high,
The dashing waters when the air is still
    From many a torrent rill
That winds unseen beneath the shaggy fell,
    Tracked by the blue mist well :
Such sounds as make deep silence in the heart
    For thought to do her part.

Tis then we hear the voice of God within,
    Pleading with care and sin :
'Child of my love ! how have I wearied thee ?
    Why wilt thou err from me ?
Have I not brought thee from the house of slaves,
    Parted the drowning waves,
And set my saints before thee in the way,
    Lest thou should'st faint or stray ?

'What ? was the promise made to thee alone ?
    Art thou the excepted one ?
An heir of glory without grief or pain ?
    O vision false and vain !

There lies thy cross ; beneath it meekly bow ;
    It fits thy stature now :
Who scornful pass it with averted eye,
    'Twill crush them by and by.

' Raise thy repining eyes, and take true measure
    Of thine eternal treasure ;
The Father of thy Lord can grudge thee nought,
    The world for thee was bought,
And as this landscape broad—earth, sea, and sky,—
    All centres in thine eye,
So all God does, if rightly understood,
    Shall work thy final good.'

CVII.

FOREST LEAVES IN AUTUMN.

RED o'er the forest peers the setting sun,
    The line of yellow light dies fast away
That crowned the eastern copse : and chill and dun
    Falls on the moor the brief November day.

Now the tired hunter winds a parting note,
    And Echo bids good-night from every glade ;
Yet wait awhile, and see the calm leaves float
    Each to his rest beneath their parent shade.

How like decaying life they seem to glide !
And yet no second spring have they in store,
But where they fall forgotten to abide,
Is all their portion, and they ask no more.

Soon o'er their heads blithe April airs shall sing,
A thousand wild-flowers round them shall unfold,
The green buds glisten in the dews of spring,
And all be vernal rapture as of old.

Unconscious they in waste oblivion lie,
In all the world of busy life around
No thought of them ; in all the bounteous sky
No drop, for them, of kindly influence found.

Man's portion is to die and rise again—
Yet he complains, while these unmurmuring part
With their sweet lives, as pure from sin and stain,
As his when Eden held his virgin heart.

And haply half unblamed his murmuring voice
Might sound in heaven, were all his second life
Only the first renewed—the heathen's choice,
A round of listless joy and weary strife.

For dreary were this earth, if earth were all,
Though brightened oft by dear Affection's kiss ;—

Who for the spangles wears the funeral pall?
　But catch a gleam beyond it, and 'tis bliss.

Heavy and dull this frame of limbs and heart,
　Whether slow creeping on cold earth, or borne
On lofty steed, or loftier prow, we dart
　O'er wave or field : yet breezes laugh to scorn

Our puny speed, and birds, and clouds in heaven,
　And fish, like living shafts that pierce the main,
And stars that shoot through freezing air at even—
　Who but would follow, might he break his chain?

And thou shalt break it soon ; the grovelling worm
　Shall find his wings, and soar as fast and free
As his transfigured Lord with lightning form
　And snowy vest—such grace he won for thee,

When from the grave he sprung at dawn of morn,
　And led through boundless air thy conquering road,
Leaving a glorious track, where saints new-born
　Might fearless follow to their blest abode.

But first, by many a stern and fiery blast
　The world's rude furnace must thy blood refine,
And many a gale of keenest woe be passed,
　Till every pulse beat true to airs divine,

Till every limb obey the mounting soul,
   The mounting soul, the call by Jesus given.
He who the stormy heart can so control
   The laggard body soon will waft to heaven.

CVIII.

CHRISTMAS EVE.

REJOICE in God alway,
   With stars in heaven rejoice,
Ere dawn of Christ's own day
   Lift up each little voice.
Look up with pure glad eye,
And count those lamps on high.
   Nay, who may count them? on our gaze
   They from their deeps come out in ever-widening
   maze.

Each in his stand aloof
   Prepares his keenest beam,
Upon that hovel roof,
   In at that door to stream,
Where meekly waits her time
The whole earth's flower and prime :—

Where in a few hours the Eternal One
Will make a clear new day, rising before the sun.

Rejoice in God alway,
  With each green leaf rejoice,
Of berries on each spray
  The brightest be your choice.
From bower and mountain lone
The autumnal hues are gone,
  Yet gay shall be our Christmas wreath,
  The glistening beads above, the burnished leaves
    beneath.

Such garland grave and fair
  His Church to-day adorns.
And—mark it well—even there
  He wears his crown of thorns.
Should aught profane draw near,
Full many a guardian spear
  Is set around, of power to go
  Deep in the reckless hand, and stay the grasping foe.

Rejoice in God alway,
  With Powers rejoice on high,
Who now with glad array
  Are gathering in the sky,

His cradle to attend,
And there all lowly bend.
  But half so low as he hath bowed
  Did never highest angel stoop from brightest cloud.

Rejoice in God alway,
  All creatures, bird and beast,
Rejoice, again I say,
  His mightiest and his least ;
From ox and ass that wait
Here on his poor estate,
  To the four living Powers, decreed
  A thousand ways at once his awful car to speed.

Rejoice in God alway :
  With saints in Paradise
Your midnight service say,
  For vigil glad arise.
Even they in their calm bowers
Too tardy find the hours
  Till he reveal the wondrous Birth :
  How must we look and long, chained here to sin and
    earth !

Ye babes, to Jesus dear,
  Rejoice in him alway.

Ye whom he bade draw near,
  O'er whom he loved to pray,
Wake and lift up the head
Each in his quiet bed.
    Listen : his voice the night wind brings ;
    He in your cradles lies, he in our carols sings.

FELICIA DOROTHEA HEMANS,
1793—1835.

CIX.

SONG IN 'THE ENGLISH MARTYRS.'

H E knelt, the Saviour knelt and prayed,
    When but his Father's eye
Looked through the lonely garden's shade
    On that dread agony ;
The Lord of all above, beneath,
Was bowed with sorrow unto death.

The sun set in a fearful hour,
    The stars might well grow dim,
When this mortality had power
    So to o'ershadow him !
That he who gave man's breath, might know
The very depths of human woe.

He proved them all,—the doubt, the strife,
    The faint perplexing dread,
The mists that hang o'er parting life,
    All gathered round his head ;
And the deliverer knelt to pray—
Yet passed it not, that cup away.

It passed not—though the stormy wave
 Had sunk beneath his tread ;
It passed not—though to him the grave
 Had yielded up its dead.
But there was sent him from on high
A gift of strength for man to die.

And was the sinless thus beset
 With anguish and dismay ?
How may we meet our conflict yet,
 In the dark narrow way ?
Through him—through him, that path who trod—
Save, or we perish, Son of God !

HENRY FRANCIS LYTE,
1793—1847.

CX.

MY BELOVED IS MINE, AND I AM HIS.

L ONG did I toil, and knew no earthly rest ;
Far did I rove, and found no certain home :
At last I sought them in his sheltering breast,
Who opes his arms, and bids the weary come.
With him I found a home, a rest divine ;
And I since then am his, and he is mine.

Yes, he is mine ! and nought of earthly things,
Not all the charms of pleasure, wealth or power,
The fame of heroes, or the pomp of kings,
Could tempt me to forego his love an hour.
'Go, worthless world,' I cry, 'with all that's thine !
Go ! I my Saviour's am, and he is mine.'

The good I have is from his stores supplied ;
The ill is only what he deems the best.
He for my friend, I'm rich with nought beside ;
And poor without him, though of all possessed.
Changes may come ; I take, or I resign,
Content, while I am his, while he is mine.

Whate'er may change, in him no change is seen,
 A glorious sun, that wanes not, nor declines ;
Above the clouds and storm he walks serene,
 And sweetly on his people's darkness shines :
All may depart ; I fret not, nor repine,
While I my Saviour's am, while he is mine.

He stays me falling, lifts me up when down,
 Reclaims me wandering, guards from every foe,
Plants on my worthless brow the victor's crown,
 Which in return before his feet I throw;
Grieved that I cannot better grace his shrine
Who deigns to own me his, as he is mine.

While here, alas ! I know but half his love,
 But half discern him, and but half adore ;
But when I meet him in the realms above,
 I hope to love him better, praise him more ;
And feel, and tell, amid the choir divine,
How fully I am his, and he is mine.

CXI.

PSALM LXXXIV.

PLEASANT are thy courts above,
    In the land of light and love ;
Pleasant are thy courts below,
In this land of sin and woe :
O ! my spirit longs and faints
For the converse of thy saints,
For the brightness of thy face,
For thy fulness, God of grace.

Happy birds, that sing and fly
Round thy altars, O Most High !
Happier souls, that find a rest
In a heavenly Father's breast !
Like the wandering dove, that found
No repose on earth around,
They can to their ark repair,
And enjoy it ever there.

Happy souls ! their praises flow
Even in this vale of woe ;
Waters in the desert rise,
Manna feeds them from the skies ;

On they go from strength to strength,
Till they reach thy throne at length ;
At thy feet adoring fall,
Who hast led them safe through all.

Lord, be mine this prize to win,
Guide me through a world of sin,
Keep me by thy saving grace ;
Give me at thy side a place.
Sun and shield alike thou art,
Guide and guard my erring heart ;
Grace and glory flow from thee :
Shower, O shower them, Lord, on me !

RICHARD THOMAS PEMBROKE POPE,
1799—1859.

WHERE dost thou feed thy favoured sheep?
    O my Beloved, tell me where ;
My soul within thy pastures keep,
    And guard me with thy tender care.
Too prone, alas ! to turn aside,
    Too prone with alien flocks to stray;
Be thou my shepherd, thou my guide,
    And lead me in thy heavenly way.

If thou would'st know, thou favoured one,
    Where soul-refreshing pastures be ;
Feed on my words of truth alone,
    And walk with those who walk with me.
I with the contrite spirit dwell ;
    The broken heart is mine abode ;
Such spikenard yields a fragrant smell,
    And such are all the saints of God.

ISAAC WILLIAMS,
1802—1865.

MUSIC.

WHAT worlds with you are come and flown !
    Musical sounds, say, what are ye?
Whence do ye come? what can ye be,
    That ye should thus our inmost being move,
Speaking with such strange language all your own?
    Are ye wild spirits, wandering from above,
That unto you such power is given?
Or are ye gales which here have strayed from heaven,
    Come from the place where all the past is stored,
    Waiting the awful coming of the Lord?
And therefore when o'er us your spirit steals
It all the past reveals,
    Finds access to the secret place of tears,
    And lifts the shadows of long-buried years
    For human tongue too deep, and human tears.

But not alone within the tuneful wall,
    And music-loving cells :—
All far aloof from spiral summit tall,
Eddying around in circuits musical,

The aerial sweetness floats and swells
Down to the woodland dells.
And wise I deem the Church of olden times
That hallowed your sweet bells, which from their towers
Flung out such spirit-moving powers,
In flood of their melodious chimes.
Well might she consecrate those fountain wells,
Such strength of sympathy within them dwells,
And keep from use profane and vile.
While now, alas ! poured forth from sacred pile,
    State strifes, home jealousies, take up the hallowed
        strain,
    And blended with the airs from hell upon the heart
    remain.

Ye golden streams from purer worlds o'erflowing,
    Musical sounds, in you a language lies,
    Which speaks of God's eternal harmonies,
In secret Providence around us going.
Ye speak as by a hidden spell
That union strange, unspeakable,
    Of the Eternal City in the skies.
Therefore in Salem's earthly courts were found,
Cymbal, lute, trumpet, harp, and vocal sound,
    And steps with music shod.
With harps angelic, songs, and hallowed lips,

Heaven is revealed in dread Apocalypse,
　Wherein the blessed spirits dwell with God.

Whate'er ye be, ye speak so much of heaven,
　That at your sound the evil spirit flies ;
　As erst we read in holy histories,
He from the stern remorseful king was driven,
　When David touched the soothing minstrelsies ;
　　The fiend then heard and caught the preludes deep
　Of sounds and thoughts harmonious, which begin
In Jesse's son,—signals precursive given　　:
　　Of that sweet music which his psalteries keep,
　Cleansing and liberating souls from sin,
　And to the everlasting refuge win.
Thus through our sensual avenues ye pour
Treasures of wisdom, truth's mysterious store
　All bathed and blended with melodious air
　Into the unwilling soul ; to harbour there
Breeding serener thoughts, in you to soar
　Above the reach of grovelling earthly care.
Therefore ye find meet place in hallowed shrine ;
Blending sweet grace with austere discipline ;
　Since that dear time when erst the shepherd throng
　　Upon that hallowed even,
　Heard strains which to angelic hosts belong,
　　As if a door were opened into heaven,
And poured a gleam of light and song,

Of glory, joy, and love eternal realms among.
   Such are the melodies of new-born Peace,
   Which then began, and will not cease
      Till men to angels shall respond, and all to praise
      be given.

Flow on, flow on, to heaven from whence ye rise,
Ye blessed harmonies,
And waft us on your breast into your parent skies ;
Attune to heaven our laggard feet,
   Attune our spirits here below
To order and obedience meet,
Such as there is in that blest seat
   From whence ye flow.

CXIV.
Elizabeth Barrett Browning,
1809—1861.

HE GIVETH HIS BELOVED, SLEEP.

OF all the thoughts of God that are
　　Borne inward into souls afar,
Along the Psalmist's music deep,
Now tell me if that any is,
For gift or grace, surpassing this—
' He giveth his beloved, sleep ' ?

What would we give to our beloved ?
The hero's heart, to be unmoved,
The poet's star-tuned harp, to sweep,
The patriot's voice, to teach and rouse,
The monarch's crown, to light the brows ?—
He giveth his beloved, sleep.

What do we give to our beloved ?
A little faith all undisproved,
A little dust to overweep,
And bitter memories to make
The whole earth blasted for our sake.
He giveth his beloved, sleep.

'Sleep soft, beloved!' we sometimes say,
But have no tune to charm away
Sad dreams that through the eyelids creep.
But never doleful dream again
Shall break the happy slumber when
He giveth his beloved, sleep.

O earth, so full of dreary noises!
O men, with wailing in your voices!
O delved gold, the wailer's heap!
O strife, O curse, that o'er it fall!
God strikes a silence through you all,
And giveth his beloved, sleep.

His dews drop mutely on the hill;
His cloud above it saileth still,
Though on its slope men sow and reap.
More softly than the dew is shed,
Or cloud is floated overhead,
He giveth his beloved, sleep.

Ay, men may wonder while they scan
A living, thinking, feeling man
Confirmed in such a rest to keep;
But angels say, and through the word
I think their happy smile is *heard*—
'He giveth his beloved, sleep.'

For me, my heart that erst did go
Most like a tired child at a show,
That sees through tears the mummers leap,
Would now its wearied vision close,
Would childlike on his love repose,
Who giveth his beloved, sleep.

And friends, dear friends,—when it shall be
That this low breath is gone from me,
And round my bier ye come to weep,
Let One, most loving of you all,
Say, 'Not a tear must o'er her fall ;
He giveth his beloved, sleep.'

HENRY ALFORD,
CXV.   1810—1871.

TRANSLATION FROM ST. BERNARD.

HAIL that head with sorrows bowing,
Crowned with thorns, with anguish flowing ;
And that body pierced and shaken,
Mocked of man, of God forsaken,
    Marred beyond the sons of men !

By thy death of life the giver,
When we suffer, O deliver !
In our sorrow and our weakness,
Thou who didst prevail by meekness,
    Think upon thy woes again !

When the hour of death is near us,
Be thou present, Lord, to cheer us ;
In that time of fear and sadness
Tarry not, our help and gladness,
    Saviour of the sons of men !

When our latest breath is failing,
Be thy Spirit all-prevailing ;
When the tempter's wiles shall prove us,
Shew thy sacred sign above us,
    Hold us, save us, free us then !

CXVI.

JOHN S. B. MONSELL,
1811—1875.

'The foxes have holes, and the birds of the air have nests ; but the Son of Man hath not where to lay his head.'

BIRDS have their quiet nest,
  Foxes their holes, and man his peaceful bed ;
All creatures have their rest,—
But Jesus had not where to lay his head.

Winds have their hour of calm,
And waves—to slumber on the voiceless deep ;
  Eve hath its breath of balm
To hush all senses, and all sounds to sleep :

The wild deer hath his lair,
The homeward flocks—the shelter of their shed ;
  All have their rest from care,—
But Jesus had not where to lay his head.

And yet he came to give
The weary and the heavy-laden rest ;
  To bid the sinner live,
And soothe our griefs to slumber, on his breast.

What then am I, my God,
Permitted thus the paths of peace to tread ?
Peace—purchased by the blood
Of him who had not where to lay his head !

I—who once made him grieve ;
I—who once bid his gentle spirit mourn ;
Whose hand essayed to weave
For his meek brow the cruel crown of thorn :—

O why should I have peace ?
Why ?—but for that unchanged, undying love,
Which would not—could not cease,
Until it made me heir of joys above.

Yes !—but for pardoning grace,
I feel I never should in glory see
The brightness of that Face,
That once was pale and agonized for me !

Let the birds seek their nest,
Foxes their holes, and man his peaceful bed ;
Come, Saviour, in my breast
Deign to repose thine oft-rejected head !

Come ! give me rest, and take
The only rest on earth thou lovest,—within
A heart, that for thy sake,
Lies bleeding, broken, penitent for sin.

CXVII.

THOMAS WHYTEHEAD,
1815—1843.

AN EASTER HYMN.

RESTING from his work to-day
In the tomb the Saviour lay ;
Still he slept, from head to feet
Shrouded in the winding-sheet,
Lying in the rock alone,
Hidden by the sealed stone.

Late at even there was seen
Watching long the Magdalene ;
Early, ere the break of day,
Sorrowful she took her way
To the holy garden glade
Where her buried Lord was laid.

So with thee, till life shall end,
I would solemn vigil spend ;
Let me hew thee, Lord, a shrine
In this rocky heart of mine,
Where in pure embalmed cell,
None but thou may ever dwell.

Myrrh and spices I will bring,
True affection's offering,
Close the door from sight and sound
Of the busy world around,
And in patient watch remain
Till my Lord appear again.

CXVIII.

JOHN MASON NEALE,
1818—1866.

TRANSLATION OF 'VENI, VENI, EMMANUEL.'

D RAW nigh, draw nigh, Emmanuel,
And ransom captive Israel,
That mourns in lonely exile here,
Until the Son of God appear ;
Rejoice ! rejoice ! Emmanuel
Shall be born for thee, O Israel '

Draw nigh, O Jesse's Rod, draw nigh,
To free us from the enemy ;
From hell's infernal pit to save,
And give us victory o'er the grave.
Rejoice ! rejoice ! Emmanuel
Shall be born for thee, O Israel !

Draw nigh, thou Orient, who shalt cheer
And comfort by thine advent here,
And banish far the brooding gloom,
Of sinful night and endless doom.
Rejoice ! rejoice ! Emmanuel
Shall be born for thee, O Israel !

Draw nigh, draw nigh, O David's Key,
The heavenly gate will ope to thee ;
Make safe the way that leads on high,
And close the path to misery.
    Rejoice ! rejoice ! Emmanuel
    Shall be born for thee, O Israel !

Draw nigh, draw nigh, O Lord of Might,
Who to thy tribes, from Sinai's height,
In ancient time didst give the law,
In cloud, in majesty, and awe.
    Rejoice ! rejoice ! Emmanuel
    Shall be born for thee, O Israel !

CXIX.

A HYMN.

O VERY God of Very God,
    And Very Light of Light,
Whose feet this earth's dark valley trod,
    That so it might be bright ;

Our hopes are weak, our fears are strong,
    Thick darkness blinds our eyes ;
Cold is the night, and O ! we long
    That thou, our Sun, would'st rise.

And even now, though dull and grey,
The east is brightening fast,
And kindling to the perfect day,
That never shall be past.

O guide us till our path is done,
And we have reached the shore
Where thou, our everlasting Sun,
Art shining evermore !

We wait in faith, and turn our face
To where the daylight springs,
Till thou shalt come our gloom to chase,
With healing in thy wings.

CXX.

AN EVENING HYMN, FROM ST. ANATOLIUS.

THE day is past and over :
All thanks, O Lord, to thee !
I pray thee now, that sinless
The hours of dark may be :
O Jesu ! keep me in thy sight,
And save me through the coming night.

The joys of day are over :
   I lift my heart to thee ;
And ask thee that offenceless
   The hours of dark may be :
O Jesu ! make their darkness light,
And save me through the coming night.

The toils of day are over ;
   I raise the hymn to thee ;
And ask that free from peril
   The hours of dark may be :
O Jesu ! keep me in thy sight,
And save me through the coming night.

Lighten mine eyes, O Saviour,
   Or sleep in death shall I ;
And he, my wakeful tempter,
   Triumphantly shall cry :
' He could not make their darkness light,
Nor guard them through the hours of night ! '

Be thou my soul's preserver,
   O God, for thou dost know
How many are the perils
   Through which I have to go :
Lover of men ! O hear my call,
And guard and save me from them all !

CXXI.

THE GUIDE, FROM 'ST. STEPHEN THE SABAITE.'

A RT thou weary, art thou languid,
    Art thou sore distrest?
'Come to me,' saith One, 'and coming
        Be at rest!'

Hath he marks to lead me to him,
    If he be my guide?
'In his feet and hands are wound-prints,
        And his side.'

Hath he diadem as monarch
    That his brow adorns?
'Yea, a crown, in very surety,
        But of thorns!'

If I find him, if I follow,
    What his guerdon here?
'Many a sorrow, many a labour,
        Many a tear.'

R

If I still hold closely to him,
  What hath he at last?
‘ Sorrow vanquished, labour ended,
          Jordan past !’

If I ask him to receive me,
  Will he say me nay?
‘ Not till earth, and not till heaven
          Pass away!’

Finding, following, keeping, struggling,
  Is he sure to bless?
‘ Angels, martyrs, prophets, virgins,
          Answer, Yes !’

THOMAS TOKE LYNCH,
1818—1871
CXXII.

LIFE.

SPIRIT ! whose various energies
    By dew and flame denoted are,
By rain from the world-covering skies,
    By rushing and by whispering air ;

Be thou to us, O gentlest one,
    The brimful river of sweet peace,
Sunshine of the celestial sun,
    Restoring air of sacred ease.

Life of our life, since life of him
    By whom we live eternally,
Our heart is faint, our eye is dim,
    Till thou our spirit purify.

The purest airs are strongest too,
    Strong to enliven and to heal :
O Spirit purer than the dew,
    Thine holiness in strength reveal.

Felt art thou, and the heavy heart
  Grows cheerful and makes bright the eyes ;
Up from the dust the enfeebled start,
  Armed and re-nerved for victories :

Felt art thou, and relieving tears
  Fall, nourishing our young resolves :
Felt art thou, and our icy fears
  The sunny smile of love dissolves.

O Spirit, when thy mighty wind
  The entombing rocks of sin hath rent,
Lead shuddering forth the awakened mind,
  In still voice whispering thine intent.

As to the sacred light of day
  The stranger soul shall trembling come,
Say, ' These thy friends,' and ' This thy way,'
  And ' Yonder thy celestial home.'

CXXIII.

A PRAYER.

O ! BREAK my heart ; but break it as a field
    Is by the plough up-broken for the corn :
O ! break it as the buds, by green leaf sealed,
  Are, to unloose the golden blossom, torn :

Love would I offer unto love's great master,
Set free the odour, break the alabaster.

O ! break my heart ; break it, victorious God,
That life's eternal well may flash abroad :
O ! let it break as when the captive trees,
Breaking cold bonds, regain their liberties :
And as thought's sacred grove to life is springing,
Be joys, like birds, their hope thy victory singing.

CXXIV.

CHRIST ON THE WATERS.

O ! WHERE is he that trod the sea,
    O ! where is he that spake,—
And demons from their victims flee,
    The dead their slumbers break ;
The palsied rise in freedom strong,
    The dumb men talk and sing,
And from blind eyes, benighted long,
    Bright beams of morning spring.

O ! where is he that trod the sea,
    O ! where is he that spake,—
And piercing words of liberty
    The deaf ears open shake ;

And mildest words arrest the haste
  Of fever's deadly fire,
And strong ones heal the weak who waste
  Their life in sad desire.

O ! where is he that trod the sea,
  O ! where is he that spake,—
And dark waves, rolling heavily,
  A glassy smoothness take ;
And lepers, whose own flesh has been
  A solitary grave,
See with amaze that they are clean,
  And cry, ' 'Tis he can save !'

O ! where is he that trod the sea,—
  'Tis only he can save ;
To thousands hungering wearily
  A wondrous meal he gave :
Full soon, celestially fed,
  Their rustic fare they take ;
'Twas springtide when he blest the bread,
  And harvest when he brake.

O ! where is he that trod the sea,—
  My soul ! the Lord is here :
Let all thy fears be hushed in thee ;
  To leap, to look, to hear,

Be thine : thy needs he'll satisfy :
Art thou diseased, or dumb ?
Or dost thou in thine hunger cry ?
' I come,' saith Christ ; ' I come.'

CXXV.

THE HEART OF CHRIST.

HEART of Christ, O cup most golden,
    Brimming with salvation's wine,
Million souls have been beholden
    Unto thee for life divine ;
Thou art full of blood the purest,
Love the tenderest and surest :
Blood is life, and life is love ;
O ! what wine is there like love ?

Heart of Christ, O cup most golden,
    Out of thee the martyrs drank,
Who for truth in cities olden
    Spake, nor from the torture shrank ;
Saved they were from traitor's meanness,
Filled with joys of holy keenness :
Strong are those that drink of love ;
O ! what wine is there like love ?

Heart of Christ, O cup most golden,
 To remotest place and time
Thou for labours wilt embolden
 Unpresuming but sublime :
Hearts are firm, though nerves be shaken,
When from thee new life is taken :
Truth recruits itself by love ;
O ! what wine is there like love ?

Heart of Christ, O cup most golden,
 Taking of thy cordial blest,
Soon the sorrowful are folden
 In a gentle healthful rest :
Thou anxieties art easing,
Pains implacable appeasing :
Grief is comforted by love ;
O ! what wine is there like love ?

Heart of Christ, O cup most golden,
 Liberty from thee we win ;
We who drink, no more are holden
 By the shameful cords of sin ;
Pledge of mercy's sure forgiving,
Powers for a holy living,—
These, thou cup of love, are thine ;
Love, thou art the mightiest wine.

EMILY BRONTÉ,
died 1849.

CXXVI.

THE OLD STOIC.

R ICHES I hold in light esteem ;
    And love I laugh to scorn ;
And lust of fame was but a dream
    That vanished with the morn :

And if I pray, the only prayer
    That moves my lips for me
Is, ' Leave the heart that now I bear,
    And give me liberty !'

Yes, as my swift days near their goal,
    'Tis all that I implore ;
In life and death, a chainless soul
    With courage to endure.

CXXVII.

STANZAS.

OFTEN rebuked, yet always back returning
   To those first feelings that were born with me,
And leaving busy chase of wealth and learning
   For idle dreams of things which cannot be :

To-day, I will seek not the shadowy region,
   Its unsustaining vastness waxes drear ;
And visions rising, legion after legion,
   Bring the unreal world too strangely near.

I'll walk, but not in old heroic traces,
   And not in paths of high morality,
And not among the half-distinguished faces,
   The clouded forms of long-past history.

I'll walk where my own nature would be leading :
   It vexes me to choose another guide :
Where the grey flocks in ferny glens are feeding ;
   Where the wild wind blows on the mountain side.

What have those lonely mountains worth revealing?
More glory and more grief than I can tell :
The earth that wakes *one* human heart to feeling
Can centre both the worlds of heaven and hell.

CXXVIII.

HER LAST LINES.

N O coward soul is mine,
No trembler in the world's storm-troubled sphere :
I see heaven's glories shine,
And faith shines equal, arming me from fear.

O God within my breast,
Almighty, ever-present Deity !
Life—that in me has rest,
As I—undying Life—have power in thee !

Vain are the thousand creeds
That move men's hearts : unutterably vain ;
Worthless as withered weeds,
Or idlest froth amid the boundless main,

To waken doubt in one
Holding so fast by thine infinity ;
So surely anchored on
The stedfast rock of immortality.

With wide-embracing love
Thy spirit animates eternal years,
Pervades and broods above,
Changes, sustains, dissolves, creates, and rears.

Though earth and man were gone,
And suns and universes ceased to be,
And thou wert left alone,
Every existence would exist in thee.

There is not room for Death,
Nor atom that his might could render void :
Thou—thou art Being and Breath,
And what thou art may never be destroyed.

CXXIX.

ARTHUR HUGH CLOUGH,
1819—1861.

QUI LABORAT ORAT.

O ONLY source of all our light and life,
  Whom as our truth, our strength, we see and feel,
But whom the hours of mortal moral strife
  Alone aright reveal !

Mine inmost soul, before thee inly brought,
  Thy presence owns ineffable, divine ;
Chastised each rebel self-encentred thought,
  My will adoreth thine.

With eye down-dropt, if then this earthly mind
  Speechless remain, or speechless e'en depart ;
Nor seek to see—for what of earthly kind
  Can see thee as thou art ?—

If well-assured 'tis but profanely bold
  In thought's abstractest forms to seem to see,
It dare not dare the dread communion hold
  In ways unworthy thee.

O not unowned, thou shalt unnamed forgive,
  In worldly walks the prayerless heart prepare ;
And if in work its life it seem to live,
  Shalt make that work be prayer.

Nor times shall lack, when while the work it plies,
  Unsummoned powers the blinding film shall part,
And scarce by happy tears made dim, the eyes
  In recognition start.

But, as thou willest, give or e'en forbear
  The beatific supersensual sight,
So, with thy blessing blest, that humbler prayer
  Approach thee morn and night.

CXXX.

O THOU whose image in the shrine
   Of human spirits dwells divine ;
Which from that precinct once conveyed,
To be to outer day displayed,
Doth vanish, part, and leave behind
Mere blank and void of empty mind,
Which wilful fancy seeks in vain
With casual shapes to fill again !

O thou that in our bosom's shrine
Dost dwell, unknown because divine !
I thought to speak, I thought to say,
' The light is here,' ' behold the way,'
' The voice was thus,' and ' thus the word,'
And ' thus I saw,' and ' that I heard,'—
But from the lips that half essayed
The imperfect utterance fell unmade.

O thou, in that mysterious shrine
Enthroned, as I must say, divine !
I will not frame one thought of what
Thou mayest either be or not.
I will not prate of ' thus ' and ' so,'
And be profane with ' yes ' and ' no,'
Enough that in our soul and heart
Thou, whatsoe'er thou may'st be, art.

Unseen, secure in that high shrine
Acknowledged present and divine,
I will not ask some upper air,
Some future day to place thee there ;
Nor say, nor yet deny, such men
And women saw thee thus and then :
Thy name was such, and there or here
To him or her thou didst appear.

Do only thou in that dim shrine,
Unknown or known, remain, divine ;
There, or if not, at least in eyes
That scan the fact that round them lies,
The hand to sway, the judgment guide,
In sight and sense thyself divide :
Be thou but there,—in soul and heart,
I will not ask to feel thou art.

It fortifies my soul to know
That, though I perish, Truth is so :
That, howsoe'er I stray and range,
Whate'er I do, thou dost not change.
I steadier step when I recall
That, if I slip, thou dost not fall.

CXXXI.

GEORGE ELIOT,
1820—1881.

LONGUM ILLUD TEMPUS QUUM NON ERO MAGIS ME MOVET QUAM HOC EXIGUUM.

O MAY I join the choir invisible
Of those immortal dead who live again
In minds made better by their presence : live
In pulses stirred to generosity,
In deeds of daring rectitude, in scorn
For miserable aims that end with self,
In thoughts sublime that pierce the night like stars,
And with their mild persistence urge man's search
To vaster issues.
            So to live is heaven :
To make undying music in the world,
Breathing as beauteous order that controls
With growing sway the growing life of man.
So we inherit that sweet purity
For which we struggled, failed, and agonised
With widening retrospect that bred despair.
Rebellious flesh that would not be subdued,
A vicious parent shaming still its child,

S

Poor anxious penitence, is quick dissolved ;
Its discords, quenched by meeting harmonies,
Die in the large and charitable air.
And all our rarer, better, truer self,
That sobbed religiously in yearning song,
That watched to ease the burthen of the world,
Laboriously tracing what must be,
And what may yet be better—saw within
A worthier image for the sanctuary,
And shaped it forth before the multitude
Divinely human, raising worship so
To higher reverence more mixed with love—
That better self shall live till human Time
Shall fold its eyelids, and the human sky
Be gathered like a scroll within the tomb,
Unread for ever.
    This is life to come,
Which martyred men have made more glorious
For us who strive to follow. May I reach
That purest heaven, be to other souls
The cup of strength in some great agony,
Enkindle generous ardour, feed pure love,
Beget the smiles that have no cruelty—
Be the sweet presence of a good diffused,
And in diffusion ever more intense.
So shall I join the choir invisible
Whose music is the gladness of the world.

Adelaide Anne Procter,
CXXXII.   1825—1864.

THANKFULNESS.

M Y God, I thank thee who hast made
    The earth so bright ;
So full of splendour and of joy,
    Beauty and light ;
So many glorious things are here,
    Noble and right !

I thank thee, too, that thou hast made
    Joy to abound ;
So many gentle thoughts and deeds
    Circling us round,
That on the darkest spot of earth
    Some love is found.

I thank thee more that all our joy
    Is touched with pain ;
That shadows fall on brightest hours ;
    That thorns remain ;
So that earth's bliss may be our guide,
    And not our chain.

For thou who knowest, Lord, how soon
    Our weak heart clings,
Hast given us joys, tender and true,
    Yet all with wings,
So that we see, gleaming on high,
    Diviner things !

I thank thee, Lord, that thou hast kept
    The best in store ;
We have enough, yet not too much
    To long for more :
A yearning for a deeper peace,
    Not known before.

I thank thee, Lord, that here our souls,
    Though amply blest
Can never find, although they seek,
    A perfect rest—
Nor ever shall, until they lean
    On Jesus' breast.

CXXXIII.

PER PACEM AD LUCEM.

I DO not ask, O Lord, that life may be
    A pleasant road ;
I do not ask that thou would'st take from me
    Aught of its load ;

I do not ask that flowers should always spring
    Beneath my feet ;
I know too well the poison and the sting
    Of things too sweet.

For one thing only, Lord, dear Lord, I plead ;
    Lead me aright—
Though strength should falter, and though heart should
    bleed—
    Through peace to light.

I do not ask, O Lord, that thou should'st shed
    Full radiance here ;
Give but a ray of peace, that I may tread
    Without a fear.

I do not ask my cross to understand,
    My way to see—
Better in darkness just to feel thy hand,
    And follow thee.

Joy is like restless day ; but peace divine
    Like quiet night :
Lead me, O Lord—till perfect day shall shine,
    Through peace to light.

INDEX OF FIRST LINES.

INDEX OF FIRST LINES.

www.ingramcontent.com/pod-product-compliance
Lightning Source LLC
Chambersburg PA
CBHW030340270326

41926CB00009B/905